THE GREEK TRAGEDY
IN NEW TRANSLATIONS

GENERAL EDITOR   William Arrowsmith

EURIPIDES: Helen

EURIPIDES
Helen

Translated by
JAMES MICHIE
and
COLIN LEACH

New York   Oxford
OXFORD UNIVERSITY PRESS
1981

Copyright © 1981 by James Michie and Colin Leach

Library of Congress Cataloging in Publication Data

Euripides.
Helen.

(The Greek tragedy in new translations)
I.* Michie, James. II. Leach, Colin.
III. Title.
PA3975.H4M5   882'.01   80-19680
ISBN 0-19-502870-8

"Palinode on Helen" by Stesichorus, translated by C. M. Bowra, from *The Oxford Book of Greek Verse in Translation*, edited by T. F. Higham and C. M. Bowra (1938), p. 214, reprinted by permission of Oxford University Press.

Medea Chorus by Euripides, translated by C. M. Bowra, from C. M. Bowra, *Periclean Athens* (1971), p. 121, reprinted by permission of Weidenfeld and Nicolson, Ltd., and Dial Press.

Printing (last digit): 987654321

Printed in the United States of America

To Ben Sonnenberg
who sees more jokes than I do

EDITOR'S FOREWORD

The Greek Tragedy in New Translations is based on the conviction that poets like Aeschylus, Sophocles, and Euripides can only be properly rendered by translators who are themselves poets. Scholars may, it is true, produce useful and perceptive versions. But our most urgent present need is for a re-creation of these plays—as though they had been written, freshly and greatly, by masters fully at home in the English of our own times. Unless the translator is a poet, his original is likely to reach us in crippled form: deprived of the power and pertinence it must have if it is to speak to us of what is permanent in the Greek. But poetry is not enough; the translator must obviously know what he is doing, or he is bound to do it badly. Clearly, few contemporary poets possess enough Greek to undertake the complex and formidable task of transplanting a Greek play without also "colonializing" it or stripping it of its deep cultural difference, its remoteness from us. And that means depriving the play of that crucial otherness of Greek experience—a quality no less valuable to us than its closeness. Collaboration between scholar and poet is therefore the essential operating principle of the series. In fortunate cases scholar and poet co-exist; elsewhere we have teamed able poets and scholars in an effort to supply, through affinity and intimate collaboration, the necessary combination of skills.

An effort has been made to provide the general reader or student with first-rate critical introductions, clear expositions of translators' principles, commentary on difficult passages, ample stage directions, and glossaries of mythical and geographical terms encountered in the plays. Our purpose throughout has been to make the reading of the plays as vivid as possible. But our poets have constantly tried to remember that they were translating plays—plays meant to be produced, in language that actors could speak, naturally and with dignity. The poetry aims at being dramatic poetry and realizing itself in words and actions that are both speakable and playable.

Finally, the reader should perhaps be aware that no pains have been spared in order that the "minor" plays should be translated as carefully and brilliantly as the acknowledged masterpieces. For the Greek Tragedy in New Translations aims to be, in the fullest sense, new. If we need vigorous new poetic versions, we also need to see the plays with fresh eyes, to reassess the plays for ourselves, in terms of our own needs. This means translations that liberate us from the canons of an earlier age because the translators have recognized, and discovered, in often neglected works, the perceptions and wisdom that make these works ours and necessary to us.

A NOTE ON THE SERIES FORMAT

If only for the illusion of coherence, a series of thirty-three Greek plays requires a consistent format. Different translators, each with his individual voice, cannot possibly develop the sense of a single coherent style for each of the three tragedians; nor even the illusion that, despite their differences, the tragedians share a common set of conventions and a generic, or period, style. But they can at least share a common approach to orthography and a common vocabulary of conventions.

1. Spelling of Greek names

Adherence to the old convention whereby Greek names were first Latinized before being housed in English is gradually disappearing. We are now clearly moving away from Latinization and toward precise transliteration. The break with tradition may be regrettable, but there is much to be said for hearing and seeing Greek names as though they were both Greek and new, instead of Roman or neo-classical importations. We cannot of course see them as wholly new. For better or worse certain names and myths are too deeply rooted in our literature and thought to be dislodged. To speak of "Helene" and "Hekabe" would be no less pedantic and absurd than to write "Aischylos" or "Platon" or

"Thoukydides." There are of course borderline cases. "Jocasta" (as opposed to "Iokaste") is not a major mythical figure in her own right; her familiarity in her Latin form is a function of the fame of Sophocles' play as the tragedy *par excellence*. And as tourists we go to Delphi, not Delphoi. The precisely transliterated form may be pedantically "right," but the pedantry goes against the grain of cultural habit and actual usage.

As a general rule, we have therefore adopted a "mixed" orthography according to the principles suggested above. When a name has been firmly housed in English (admittedly the question of domestication is often moot), the traditional spelling has been kept. Otherwise names have been transliterated. Throughout the series the -os termination of masculine names has been adopted, and Greek diphthongs (as in Iphigeneia) have normally been retained. We cannot expect complete agreement from readers (or from translators, for that matter) about borderline cases. But we want at least to make the operative principle clear: to walk a narrow line between orthographical extremes in the hope of keeping what should not, if possible, be lost; and refreshing, in however tenuous a way, the specific sound and nameboundedness of Greek experience.

2. *Stage directions*

The ancient manuscripts of the Greek plays do not supply stage directions (though the ancient commentators often provide information relevant to staging, delivery, "blocking," etc.). Hence stage directions must be inferred from words and situations and our knowledge of Greek theatrical conventions. At best this is a ticklish and uncertain procedure. But it is surely preferable that good stage directions should be provided by the translator than that the reader should be left to his own devices in visualizing action, gesture, and spectacle. Obviously the directions supplied should be both spare and defensible. Ancient tragedy was austere and "distanced" by means of masks, which means that the reader must not expect the detailed intimacy ("He shrugs and turns wearily away." "She speaks with deliberate slowness, as though to emphasize the point," etc.) which characterizes stage directions in modern naturalistic drama. Because Greek drama is highly rhetorical and stylized, the translator knows that his words must do the real work of inflection and nuance. Therefore every effort has been made to supply the visual and tonal sense required by a given scene and the reader's (or actor's) putative unfamiliarity with the ancient conventions.

3. Numbering of lines

For the convenience of the reader who may wish to check the English against the Greek text or vice versa, the lines have been numbered according to both the Greek text and the translation. The lines of the English translation have been numbered in multiples of ten, and these numbers have been set in the right-hand margin. The (inclusive) Greek numeration will be found bracketed at the top of the page. The reader will doubtless note that in many plays the English lines outnumber the Greek, but he should not therefore conclude that the translator has been unduly prolix. In most cases the reason is simply that the translator has adopted the free-flowing norms of modern Anglo-American prosody, with its brief, breath- and emphasis-determined lines, and its habit of indicating cadence and caesuras by line length and setting rather than by conventional punctuation. Other translators have preferred four-beat or five-beat lines, and in these cases Greek and English numerations will tend to converge.

4. Notes and Glossary

In addition to the Introduction, each play has been supplemented by Notes (identified by the line numbers of the translation) and a Glossary. The Notes are meant to supply information which the translators deem important to the interpretation of a passage; they also afford the translator an opportunity to justify what he has done. The Glossary is intended to spare the reader the trouble of going elsewhere to look up mythical or geographical terms. The entries are not meant to be comprehensive; when a fuller explanation is needed, it will be found in the Notes.

ON THE TRANSLATORS

Colin Leach studied Classics at Oxford University in the fifties and, following his first degrees, became a Classical Tutor at Brasenose College, specializing in Ancient Drama. After spending a number of years in the City of London, he returned to Oxford in 1979, where he is now a Fellow of Pembroke College. He is the author of numerous articles and reviews on a wide variety of classical subjects; and at present he is occupied with a study of Aristophanic comedy. He is one of the relatively few remaining regular composers in Greek and Latin verse.

His collaborator, James Michie, is presently a Director of the Bodley Head in London. He holds an M.A. in Classics and English Literature from Oxford University. His publications include a book of poems, *Possible Laughter* (1959), and translations of various Latin poets, *The Odes of Horace, The Poems of Catullus,* and *The Epigrams of Martial.* He has also edited *The Bodley Head Book of Longer Short Stories,* and, most recently, translated *Selected Fables of La Fontaine.*

ON THE TRANSLATION

"It is all iridescence," observed a contemporary French scholar of Euripides' *Helen.* He was speaking descriptively, not impressionistically. In the whole Euripidean corpus, there is nothing quite like this play, with its glittering wit, its ingenuity of contrivance and elegance of execution, and, at a deeper level, its subtext of tragedy and pain and the pathos of the impossible. At every point, the sensitive reader will feel the dramatist's delight in his own virtuosity, in his ability to "dance in the chains of convention," outwitting, if not outraging, expectation with constant surprising peripeties. Like *Orestes* and *Ion,* the *Helen* is a complex tissue of sustained and often contrasting reversals whose dramatic effect is the sense of something unstated or unrevolved at the very heart of things, an ellipsis or enigma in reality itself. The reader feels the presence of a design in the unfolding rhythm of the obviously patterned reversals of dramatic events; but when he asks himself the meaning of the design, it slips away, as though the point were mysteriously suppressed or missing.

The play refuses to resolve the problems raised by its own patterned reversals. And the reader feels this apparent absence of resolution as dissonance. In this respect, of course, the *Helen* is like many other Euripidean plays in which the essential structural principle is the systematic contrasting of different "worlds," different orders of reality. Again and again Euripides sets the ideal against the real, or the real against the ideal; the tragic against the comic-romantic or comic-pathetic; literary epic and high poetry against ordinary everyday reality; archaic against contemporary; the reality of "things as they are said to be" (myth or *logos*) against "things as they are" (actuality, fact, *ergon*). The result is the sense of consistent, even studied anachronism, which one finds everywhere in Euripides. The dramatist obviously takes pains to produce the sense of cultural clash, the dissonance in values, that necessarily results from juxtaposing these opposed "worlds" or realities. The mythical or ideal (not necessarily synonymous, at least in Euripides) values of the culture are set against its actual values (often nobler, but often more base than the ideal values), and the effect is inevitably that of a world where things are deliberately prevented from "phasing," from converging and integrating. The world, in short, as it must have seemed to Euripides in the last thirty years of the fifth century.

But in the *Helen* (and the *Orestes*), this principle is pushed to its logical, or perhaps illogical, extreme. Here we have, in the form of a palinodic recantation of Euripides' persistent disparagement of Helen elsewhere,[1] a denial of the "tragic" Helen by contrast with an invented "romantic" Helen of surpassing domestic virtue. Helen, we are told, did not go to Troy; she was abducted to Egypt where, after the Trojan War, the shipwrecked Menelaos finds her, her virtue besieged by an amorous Egyptian prince. Between these two Helens, the tragic adulteress of epic and the "retouched" Helen of our play, the poet seemingly invites his audience to choose. But in one sense—the crucial sense, I think—there is really no choice; or rather, the choice is merely apparent, a device *ex hypothesi* by which Euripides obliquely but firmly drives home his point—the utter futility of the Trojan (i.e. Peloponnesian) War. The palinodic fiction intensifies the tragedy of the war by demonstrating its futility, a war fought for the possession of a phantom. Helen—whoever "Helen" may be—is rehabilitated, but the result is to assert even more strongly the meaningless suffering of all those thousands who fought and died for ten long years to bring her home. In the end, the phantom who went to Troy is more real—more symbolically real, above all in her effect upon others—than the palinodic "flesh-and-blood" Helen of the play.

Of what is Helen a symbol? What else but that figure of lethally intoxicating loveliness that, in play after play, floats across the Euripidean stage, luring men to their destruction in pursuit of a

---

1. See, for instance, *The Trojan Women* or *Hecuba*, where Hecuba exclaims of her doomed daughter Polyxena, "O gods,/ to see there, in her place, Helen of Sparta,/ sister of the sons of Zeus, whose lovely eyes made ashes of the happiness of Troy!"

will-o'-the-wisp, the objectification of their own desire. "What *Aphrodite* has driven this army mad?", asks a character in another play, and he means: mad with desire, with the lust known to his contemporaries as *eros*: the lust for power, empire, wealth, conquest. *Libido dominandi.* Helen is Euripides' image of what Thucydides called *archē*, the power of rule which the historian regarded as the effective cause of the Peloponnesian War, and which Aristophanes personified in the *Birds* as *Basileia* ("sovereignty," "rule," the reward which Pisthetairos, the winged imperialist of Cloudcuckooland, claims from Zeus as his right).[2]

The play is, as Colin Leach suggests, profoundly pacifist, a dramatic prayer as it were, almost a spell, to bring the "true" Helen home to Hellas where she belongs, out of foreign parts. "Foreign parts" will mean of course many things: Syracuse, where the great Athenian armada was already doomed; all those distant places in which the Athenians—in Thucydides' powerfully compact phrase, *duserōtes tōn apontōn*, "unlucky lovers of distant (i.e. unobtainable) things"—had sought to extend their unappeasable hunger for empire; or perhaps that underworld from which Demeter and all Hellenes hungered to repatriate the lost Persephone. Whatever else this play may be about, it is surely not the "escapism" which has been so persistently attributed to it (and, with equal improbability, to Aristophanes' *Birds*).

Translating such a play is ticklish high-wire work. For obvious reasons. One mis-step, and the whole airy artifice crumbles. If the translator miscalculates the timing or the intricate involutions of the reversals at the instant of their pivoting; if he misconstrues the tone or tension by overstressing real or ideal, tragic or romantic; if he fails to register the delicate inflections of character, then the play loses, if not quite everything, at least that sure-footed acrobatic balance on which its beauty depends. At every point the play challenges the translator to preserve the *texture.* For the texture embodies the dramatist's sense of the actual texture of human experience generally but above all *at the time*: life lived in the shuddering tension between real and ideal, between what men are and what they might aspire to be; between their own inconsistent

---

2. See *Birds*, 1536-41. Aristophanes plays punningly on the word *basíleia* (princess, queen), which is thereupon glossed (by Prometheus) in the sense of *basileíā* (sovereignty, power, etc.): "She [Basileia] is the stewardess of Zeus's thunder and of everything else, good counsel, good government, restraint, naval arsenals, slander, paymasters, and judicial payments too."

natures, at once animal and divine, and the uncertain and perhaps unknowable purposes of gods represented so vividly in the reversals by which human existence is rhythmed, now for better, now for worse. To these extremely taxing demands, it seems to me that the translators have responded with consistent tact of understanding and poetic skill.

One last point of important disagreement. In his Introduction, Colin Leach argues that the play abounds in signs of hasty composition. There are, no doubt, inconsistencies. But none of these, it seems to me, amounts to much when set against the astonishing technical control exhibited by the poet, above all in tone and texture—matters in which the poet's care and intelligence are evident throughout. Theonoë may not have been consulted by Helen because Helen, like the Servant, is perhaps as skeptical about prophecy as she is about her own mythological background ("There's an old story . . . which may or may not be true"). In the recognition-scene I see no problem whatever; it is handled with great technical agility, and it enjoyed, I suppose (given Aristophanes' parody of it), great popular success at the time. The Demeter ode admittedly poses real problems. But if we suppose, as we reasonably may,[3] that the *Iphigeneia at Tauris* was performed as a third play in the same group with *Helen* and the (lost) *Andromeda* in 412 B.C., the problem largely dissolves. That is, the extremely close structural resemblances between the *Iphigeneia at Tauris* and the *Helen* then appear, not as structural self-plagiarism by Euripides, but unmistakable linking by means of coordinate—i.e. corresponding—structural units or actions (the recognition-scene, the escape, epiphany, etc.).[4] And since all three plays deal with the theme of *la perduta ritrovata* (in every case a Greek girl, lost or abducted or constrained by barbarians, is rescued and repatriated by a Greek hero), the beautiful ode telling of Demeter's anguished search for her own lost child, the ravished Persephone, with its ritual theme of loss and recovery, death and rebirth, falls into thematic place, linking the three plays to a

3. Cf. A. M. Dale, ed., *Euripides Helen* (Oxford, 1967), xxiv-xxviii, for a different view. Dale believes that the *Iph. Taur.* is to be dated to 414, two years before the *Helen*. But her evidence is entirely metrical. And while such evidence is invaluable for dating Euripides' plays to distinct periods, metrical criteria are no better than carbon-14 dating for pinpoint-accuracy. Nor, it seems to me, can structural arguments be so easily dismissed.

4. See Richmond Lattimore's Introduction to his translation of *Iph. Taur.* in this series (Oxford, 1973).

larger mythological pattern of return, deliverance, and redemption. The great dramatist deserves the benefit of the critical doubt, even the doubts of his admirers. To no Euripidean play does Goethe's observation apply more accurately, I believe, than to the *Helen:* "Over the scenes of Hellas and its primitive body of legends he sails and swims like a cannonball in a sea of mercury and cannot sink even if he tries. . . ."

Baltimore and New York   William Arrowsmith

CONTENTS

HELEN

INTRODUCTION

Of the eighteen or nineteen plays of Euripides which have reached us in complete form, is any more elusive than *Helen?* Is it a tragedy, a comedy, a dramatic exercise in philosophy (a kind of remote prototype of Beckett's *Waiting for Godot* or Tom Stoppard's *Jumpers*), a thoroughly perverse *ballon d'essai*, a play written for, and for performance by, women only—or what? The clues exist, but the labyrinth is tortuous and the answer multi-faceted.

First, then, this is one of Euripides' later plays; it was produced, probably at the city Dionysia, in 412 B.C. (a date which, exceptionally, can be taken as certain). He was as fertile as ever, with *Orestes*, *Phoenissae*, and, above all, *Bacchae* still to emerge; indeed, in fifty years he was to compose nearly ninety plays. A date can mean much, a little, nothing; this one, 412 B.C., does (as I shall shortly argue) mean a lot. For, even if there is no need to recount here the dismal story of incompetence, procrastination, and ill-fortune which led to the calamitous defeat of the Athenians' huge (and then reinforced) expedition to Sicily, let us at least remember that the final catastrophes, by sea and land, took place in autumn of 413 B.C. 412 B.C. was not an easy nor an agreeable year for the Athenians, who had now been at war with Sparta, almost continuously, for nineteen years.

Next, Helen herself. The dramatist, to be fair, gives us warning of surprises to come; in the very first line he tells us, through Helen, that we are to imagine ourselves as being on the banks of the Nile: we are in a remote and unfamiliar country, where anything could happen, and anything might be expected. Egypt

3

then—though far from unknown, of course—was still a distant land, difficult of access, full of marvels. A few lines later, and we are being introduced to Proteus: not the well-known Proteus of Homer, who had the gift of turning himself at will into other species, but quite a different one, a king of Egypt. Another few lines, and Helen is casting doubt (18-22*), in rather a sly fashion, on the story surrounding her own birth:

There's an old story that Zeus changed himself
into a swan once and, being chased by an eagle,
flew to my mother Leda's lap for refuge
and by trick got what he wanted from her—
which may or may not be true.

What *sort* of Helen is heroine of this play will emerge as the plot develops; what the audience has first to cope with is the realization that Euripides' play is based on the violent variation of the myth which is ascribed to the Sicilian poet Stesichorus. Stesichorus was a lyric poet who flourished in the first half of the sixth century B.C. Legend, as recounted by Plato, claimed that, after he had told the conventional version of Helen's story, he was blinded: after all, she was by now regarded as a goddess, at least in Sparta. Hence, the famous *Palinode*, with its best-known lines:

It is not true, this tale,
You never once set sail
On well-benched ships, nor went
To Troy's tall battlement.
(TR. C. M. BOWRA)

Of course, too much violence to the myth would be unacceptable; hence Stesichorus seems to have invented the phantom-Helen, or "eidōlon," who "really" went to Troy while the real-live Helen stayed with Proteus in Egypt. Further particulars about Helen's stay in Egypt are provided by Herodotus in his narrative of Egyptian history, and some of this is used by Euripides—but the most important elements of the plot are unquestionably the invention of the dramatist.

For the unusual version of the myth, a Helen to match. In the tradition to which Athenian playgoers were—or, for that matter, modern playgoers are—accustomed, Helen was "one of the su-

* Unless otherwise indicated, line references throughout are to the English translation.

preme figures of Greek mythology, daughter of Zeus and radiant exemplar of the power of Aphrodite, the living symbol of all men's desires for beauty, married to men of a little less than heroic stature, sinning and bringing destruction to a city and death to thousands, yet herself curiously unscathed and undimmed by it all." So, justly, A. M. Dale;[1] and perhaps we shall think of those lines in the *Iliad* where the Trojan elders, seeing Helen walking on the walls of Troy, said, "Who on earth could blame the Trojan and Achaean warriors for suffering so long for such a woman's sake? Indeed, she is the very image of an immortal goddess." To be sure, later authors were sometimes less kind. For example, viciously and deliberately punning in a chorus of the *Agamemnon*, Aeschylus described her as "Hell to ships, hell to cities, hell to men." But in this play there is nothing of that. Here we have a wife of total faithfulness—yes, after seventeen years!— wronged by the gods and men. She cuts off her hair to feign mourning—she even wishes she looked plainer (277-78); she is positively agreeable to Menelaos, while being only too obviously (to us, not to him) very much cleverer than he is. She is already worried about the prospective spinsterhood of her daughter Hermione. She is altogether very different from the standard Helen who had appeared, only three years earlier, as a character of middling importance, in *The Trojan Women*. In *The Trojan Women*, Helen is faced with imminent death, after the fall of Troy, at the hands of Menelaos. She remains unmoved and dignified; well may Hecuba warn Menelaos not to fall once again under her spell, she "who snares the eyes of men." To Hecuba, Helen is the Queen of Love, and she comments bitterly on the similarity of the words "sensual" and "senseless" (in Greek, *Aphroditē* and *aphrosynē*). The most recent editor of the play says that Menelaos "treats Helen with apparent contempt. Beneath this veneer his true feelings can be seen. Helen's beauty is too much for him and we feel sure that it will finally prevail."[2] Even if so much can hardly be extracted from the text, this is fair comment; for our purpose we need only note that there is nothing in this, the accepted, picture of Helen (and Menelaos) that would have alerted Athenian playgoers to the idea of a totally different Helen just three years later. We are, in brief, dealing with the standard version of the myth.

1. *Helen* (Oxford, 1967), p. vii.
2. K. H. Lee (London, 1975), p. xxv.

It is quite clear that the treatment in *Helen* was startling. We have a tantalizing glimpse of just how startling it was from the sure-footed Aristophanes. In the very next year, 411 B.C., Aristophanes produced his *Thesmophoriazūsae*, or *Women at a Religious Festival*. This play is exceptional in that it contains a prolonged parody of the *Helen*, including many direct quotations. This is inconceivable unless our play had secured speedy and widespread acclaim—or at least notoriety. And, even more to the point, in the passage which introduces the parody, the speaker (Mnēsilochus) says, as he wonders how to bring Euripides to his assistance, "I know; I'll imitate the new *Helen*"—where the Greek work for "new," *kainos*, means not only "recent" but "newfangled."

Nothing, then, is as it seems or as we should expect it to be in a well-ordered universe. Appearance is to be contrasted with reality—and frequently contrasted: by my count nearly 30 times in less than 1700 lines. We have set off on the long road, though we have not yet realised it, to the New Comedy, to Menander and his sets of identical twins, to the *Menaechmi* of Plautus, to *The Comedy of Errors*.

This is (as A. W. Verrall[3] saw) a woman's play. Verrall's insights were none the less real for being flawed; and while we need not accept his theories concerning the *Helen*, for all their brilliant expression, either in whole or in part—indeed, who ever has accepted them?—we shall assuredly accept that women have the best parts in both dramatic and moral terms. Take the men: Teucer? Little more than a blustering substitute for a program, he appears from nowhere, shortly to vanish, his purpose unachieved, into that same nowhere whence he came. Theoklymenos, who makes a brief, but unappealing, appearance toward the end, has small opportunity to shine, being hardly more than the personification of a threat. Menelaos himself, the brother of the great Agamemnon, cuts a dismal figure. Tattered and cowering on first appearance, he accepts being browbeaten by a servant (how Thersites would have enjoyed *that!*); he is slow in the uptake and impractical in invention: in short, anything but a hero. By contrast, the women all come out well: the portress who worsts Menelaos; the priestess Theonöe with her "shrine of justice" in her heart, in whose hands lies the safety of Helen and

3. *Four Plays of Euripides* (Cambridge, England, 1905), pp. 43-133.

Menelaos; and, of course, Helen herself, the home and husband-loving Helen, faithful, ingenious, practical, never-despairing.

At this point, a brief summary of the plot becomes essential. Helen, seated as a suppliant on the tomb of Proteus, is anxious to avoid a forced marriage with his son Theoklymenos, whose sister is Theonöe, the omniscient prophetess. Teucer enters to consult Theonöe (how did he know she was available?), but instead has a horrified exchange with the woman who, to him, is exactly like the hated Helen. Teucer tells Helen of the events at Troy before departing, his purposes not achieved, at the threat of the arrival of Theoklymenos. In the next scene, Menelaos makes his ship-wrecked appearance, dressed (according to Aristophanes) in a piece of sailcloth—it is here that he has his discreditable episode with the portress. In due course, Helen and the Chorus emerge to join him, now knowing from Theonöe that Menelaos is indeed alive. Menelaos, who has arrived in Egypt accompanied by the Helen-*eidōlon*, understandably finds the situation puzzling, and does not accept the real Helen for what she is until he hears of the disappearance, in surprising circumstances, of the phantom. Plans for escape—or, failing that, suicide—are made, but all depends upon the silence of Theonöe. Theonöe hears the pleas of Helen and Menelaos, and is persuaded to silence; the pair finally decide to trick Theoklymenos by pretending that Menelaos is dead (so that a ship can be provided for Helen in which to perform the funeral rites). The rest of the play is occupied with the successful execution of the plan; a passage between Menelaos and Theoklymenos in which the former purports to be one of his own crew provides yet more opportunity for *double entendre* and dramatic irony. The curtain is rung down, suitably enough, by an appearance *ex machina* by Helen's brothers, Kastor and Polydeukes; and all ends happily.

So bald a narrative, though it can convey nothing of the language—serious, blustering, matter-of-fact, philosophical, moralizing, comic, or whatever—at least leaves us in no doubt that *Helen* is not, and cannot be in any "traditional" sense, a tragedy—if by "tragedy" we think of the *Agamemnon* or *Oedipus Rex* or *Bacchae*. To be sure, Richmond Lattimore makes a partly valid point when he says, listing the striking similarities between *Iphigeneia in Tauris* and *Helen*, "The occasion and sanctions of performance, the use of heroic legend, the tragic diction and meters, the tragic actors, costumes, and every circumstance defined it as tragedy, and the happy ending made no difference."[4] But there is, perhaps, some risk of circularity of argument here, which, if accepted, would make it difficult for a dramatist to be allowed to develop except within disagreeably narrow confines; moreover, *Helen* shows, at times, a striking informality of diction—there's a good example at one point when the messenger, seeing one (real) Helen and believing her to be the other (*eidōlon*, real-to-him) Helen, says, in effect, "Oh, hello Helen—so you *were* here, after all." Again, we have seen that Euripides is using an unfamiliar version of the myth; and we can be certain that Menelaos' costume at least was of an outré appearance. There is a feeling of experiment throughout the play, difficult to communicate except by lengthy quotation—so that one may sympathize with Lattimore, who advised his readers to read *Helen* before reading his introduction to it. Perhaps, however, modern received opinion has gone too far in the other direction: the late Professor T. B. L. Webster wrote:[5]

The *Helen* should not be taken too seriously: it is gay, often exciting, sometimes comic, always beautiful. The story of the eidōlon makes nonsense of the Trojan War, and both the old servant and the chorus touch on this theme. No doubt Euripides believes that quarrels should be settled by argument rather than by battle, and that commonsense is more useful than prophecy, but he treats this very lightly. . . . He has simply accepted the eidōlon story and written a very pretty play on its consequences.

This seems a long way too dismissive. To begin with, it takes no account of the play's philosophizing, its emphasis on the meaning of words, the constant harping on the sophistic distinction between *onoma* (name = appearance) and *logos* (word) on the one hand, and *sōma* (body), *prāgma* (fact, reality), or *ergon* (fact) on the other. One thinks of Menelaos' bafflement on the possibility of two Zeuses co-existing, two Helens, two Troys (511-18):

> Is there a man
> by the name of Zeus living beside the Nile?
> No, for there's one Zeus only—the one in heaven.
> And where else in the world can there be a Sparta
> except beside the reed-bright, rippling Eurotas?

4. *Iphigeneia in Tauris* (New York, 1973), p. 5.
5. *The Tragedies of Euripides* (London, 1967), pp. 201-02.

. . . Can there possibly be a second Sparta *and* another Troy?

Commentators have observed other sophistic associations, notably a use of *reductio ad impossibile* which may even derive from Gorgias. Again, in famous lines (1089-91) Theonöe speaks of the notion of the survival after death of a spiritual element in mankind; and this—like a somewhat similar passage in Euripides' *Suppliants*[6]—early led to the noting of the relationship between Euripides and Anaxagoras:

The dead may not have living minds like ours,
but having once mixed with immortal ether
they have immortal consciousness.

So much, perhaps, is reasonably clear, relatively interesting: Euripides in old age was no less willing to experiment, no less willing to listen to the latest offerings of the philosophers. But an important paper by Charles Segal, entitled "The Two Worlds of Euripides' *Helen*," has taken this much further, by demonstrating the depth and complexity of the underlying philosophical structure. Segal's study, one of the most penetrating and authoritative discussions of the play, may in a few instances go a little further than the evidence, strictly speaking, permits; that is, in any case, unimportant. What he shows is that the play contains a whole pattern of antitheses that goes far beyond the onoma-prāgma contacts: for example, death and life; true inner piety and outward regard for religious forms; cosmic perspective and narrow possessiveness; feminine values and masculine values; and, of course, peace and war. Segal develops his theme by taking three main generic contrasts—Reality and Appearance, Helen and Menelaos, and Theonöe and Theoklymenos—and developing the underlying antitheses from there. His analysis concludes:

The issue of whether the play is comedy or tragedy is, in the last analysis, irrelevant. Euripides, like many artists in the late stages of their work, has created a form which transcends the precise limits between genres. Shakespeare's late "tragic" romances—notably *Cymbeline* and *Pericles*—are a close analogy. The urge and the encouragement to go beyond the conventional form of tragedy must have come with the conception of the basic material of the plot: the complex interchanges of appearance and reality, the exotic setting, the philosophical mysticism, the ritual death and rebirth, the odes on Perse-

6. Gilbert Murray, ed. (Oxford Classical Texts, 1913), ll. 531-34.

phone and the Mountain mother, the blend of sophistic epistemology and ancient, Odyssean archetypes. The equally "romantic" and "comic" features of plays like the *Iphigeneia Among the Taurians* and the *Ion*—to say nothing of the heroless *Trojan Women* or the tripartite *Herakles*—suffice to show that Euripides was in a period of intense artistic exploration.[7]

It is Segal's achievement that, among much else, he has given back to *Helen* its claim as a deeply serious play—a claim which even Wilamowitz would not and did not accept. By so doing, as I shall maintain, he has opened the way to an interpretation of *Helen* which will enable its title as a "tragedy" to be restored, even if in an indirect and unexpected way.

In lines 972-77 (significantly, the lines not only are spoken by Helen to Theonöe, but also appear just after the play is halfway through) Helen says:

God abominates violence; his commandment
to all of us is: get and enjoy possessions,
but not by robbery. For just as the sky
belongs to all men, so too does this earth
where each may fill his house with goods, so long as
they are his own, and not snatched from his neighbor.

In the context, where Helen is actually talking of her position vis-à-vis Theoklymenos, the lines had enough of a gnomic feel about them to ensure their elimination, in some editions, from the text. Nothing could be less likely.

We can now no longer ignore the political background in which *Helen* made its appearance. Few among its audience did not have a relation who had been a casualty (whether dead or imprisoned) of the Sicilian Expedition; demographers have even asserted that perhaps one-quarter of free Athenian males of military age were so lost. This was the greatest single disaster in Athens' imperial history; worse, it could not possibly be imputed to virtuous motivation. Not for nothing, in Thucydides' *History*, does the account of the Sicilian Expedition *immediately* follow the appalling story of Athens' despicably cruel treatment of Melos. For the Athenian invasion of Sicily was nakedly devoted to gain at the expense of others, to win (as we might put it nowadays) the foreign currency, especially in terms of gold, that

7. *Transactions of the American Philological Association* (TAPA), 102 (1971), pp. 553-614.

would enable them to carry on the war against Sparta with a growing rather than a dwindling band of allies.

The expedition failed, failed catastrophically. Then is the *Helen* an "anti-war tract"? It appeared less than a year after the Sicilian disaster, at a time when it would be absurdly weak to say that questions of the war's likely outcome and usefulness were "in the air." Yet the play itself contains relatively little that can be interpreted, directly or indirectly, as an attack on war—though we must note that the play's most obvious direct attack on anything, divination, has immediate relevance to the craze for just that, which, in an outburst of superstition, broke out at exactly that time; as Thucydides tells us in his usual clinical language. And that craze seems to have been particularly connected, not surprisingly, with the fate of the Sicilian Expedition. A servant says (806-21):

> I do now see
> how full of lies, how rotten the whole business
> of prophecy is. . . . Much better
> to sacrifice and pray to the gods and leave
> prophets alone. Prophecy was invented
> as a bait for gullible man, but no one ever
> got rich without hard work by studying magic.

Indeed, the passage chimes a little oddly in a play where so important a role is played by the priestess/prophetess Theonöe: this suggests that Euripides badly wanted to get it off his chest. One anti-war passage indeed there is: in the second antistrophe of the third choric ode we read (1240-52):

> Madmen, all who seek glory in war,
> trusting in ignorance
> to the sheer weight of the lance
> to end mortal debate!
> If battle and blood are to settle the score,
> grief and hate
> will never leave the cities of men. Through strife
> such men have found
> cramped sleeping room, a Trojan burial mound,
> who might by words have learnt
> some way to compound
> the quarrel over Menelaos' wife—
> you, Helen!

(Unsurprising sentiments, it may be felt, from the author of the elegy for the Athenians who fell in Sicily.) Here the voice of the pacifist comes through loud and clear, but in a relatively harmless place. (The other choric odes provide little or nothing of substance, and, as A. M. Dale aptly observes of the first of them, "like many of the songs in Helen this is an operatic aria whose words must not be expected to bear too close a scrutiny of their meaning.")

Supporting evidence exists, but it must be used with due caution. Suppose, for a moment, that Helen was, in a valid sense, a reaction to the Sicilian expedition's failure, then there was not much time to write it. Bad news reaches Athens, autumn, 413 B.C.; Helen written, and rehearsed, 413/12 B.C.; Helen produced: city Dionysia, roughly end-March, 412 B.C. In such a case, one would expect evidence of hasty composition to exist. It not only exists: it abounds.

The play rests upon the shaky substructure of a giant fault; a fault which Euripides will have recognized, but (since he was not writing for pedants 2,400 years later) will have ignored. Theonöe is omniscient, we learn immediately; yet for seventeen years Helen has not bothered to consult her, whether as to the Trojan War, or the fate of Menelaos, or the prospects of her eventual reunion with him. Of course, Euripides may have felt that such a detail would readily be passed over (more likely, not noticed at all during performance) by the audience: but there is more, as soon as one starts looking.

First, the Teucer episode. It is held to presage the arrival, later on, of Menelaos; but it contains nothing that a (character-eliminating) dialogue with, say, Theonöe could not have conveyed. Next, the recognition (anagnōrisis): two attempts at this have to be made, and one may (or may not) believe that what we have is an imperfect conflation of two attempts to achieve, in a difficult philosophical context, a satisfactory synthesis. There is much minor evidence, but it is technical in the sense that, while arguable, it depends on knowledge of both Greek and Greek stagecraft; better to look at one more major point of concern to critics.

The final choric ode of the play, generally known as the "Great Mother" or "Mountain Mother" ode, has long been a source of worry to scholars. Choric odes are "supposed" to be related, even if remotely, to the general themes of the play; in this case, ingenuity has been forced to its limits. Demeter is (but the text is sadly corrupt) distressed at the loss of her daughter. What on earth (or elsewhere) has this got to do with Helen? One can hardly blame A. W. Verrall for claiming that this ode helps to prove that *Helen* was first performed at a festival when rites attended only by women were performed in honor of the Greek Mother Demeter, and her daughter Persephone. Another, less sensitive, suggestion can be advanced: *Helen* needed another choric ode at about this point (as a play it is unevenly balanced between scenes, which must have put considerable strain on the three actors allowed by convention); may not Euripides, in some haste, have inserted an ode from his reservoir? After all, if our argument has any force, it was not the *choruses* where his message was likely to lie.

Lastly, we have already drawn attention to the fact of the close comparison with *Iphigeneia in Tauris*; and, once again, an explanation obtrudes itself—Euripides' willingness to use another framework, and available material, to ease the rapid production of a play where he was more concerned with the message than the medium. Haste would explain (if not excuse) much that has for long exercised the attention of critics; while, from the pedantic point of view, a number of lines which have been rejected as spurious on grounds of context, taste, meter, or Greek might just possibly, on the basis of the argument we have advanced, be reprieved. It is at this point that we must look for more direct support from the play itself—or in its motif. And it stares us in the face.

Of course, it is not the *theme*, but the *starting-point*, of *Helen* that the Greeks and Trojans went to war for ten years over a phantom—a war which Thucydides himself, in the opening chapters of his *History*, is far from decrying in terms of importance. A *phantom!* Euripides was not writing for fools, and no underlining would have been necessary for his audience to consider that, just possibly, another people was, even now, at war in search of a different sort of phantom. In any case, a more direct approach would have been at best imprudent. Euripides (it is said) had already suffered arrest and impeachment—possibly on political grounds—"impiety" being the charge; he was far too subtle a person, and dramatist, to run any such risk needlessly again. There is no hint of subversion in *Helen*—except to those who, by alleging it, would *ex hypothesi* have admitted the existence of aggression and the corruption of greed. Naturally, even in Euripides, not everything is perfectly carried out: there are frigidities in Aeschylus, and bad jokes in Aristophanes, just as Homer nods. In *Helen*, there is much that is, in one way or another, imperfect; but if (and it cannot be so very unlikely) we suppose that he wanted to produce a play with relevance to Athens' morally and (nearly) physically bankrupt situation, and produce it in great haste, then perhaps we have the plausible outcome: much intellectual depth and brilliance, but imperfect stagecraft.

Nor, of course, does this mean that the arguments advanced by Charles Segal are in any way irrelevant. Rather, their relevance is heightened: and the themes are always contrast and comparison. The Trojan War was fought over a phantom: for what, precisely, after nineteen years, was the Peloponnesian War being fought? Was Sicily's gold real, or another phantom? Did the public attitude of Athens—as best seen by us in the account given by Thucydides of Pericles' speeches—really accord with its real-world behavior? Or did even Athenians say one thing and do another? If we even begin to accept that thoughts like these were in Euripides' mind when he wrote *Helen*, then we should also feel that it no longer makes sense to ask whether the play is "technically" a tragedy, or a comedy, or a vehicle for philosophical expression, or anything else. It is all of these, and the philosophical content may have been partly serious, partly camouflage (who can tell?): but it is something much more than any of these things, something that should appeal to us more nearly than the appalling destiny of the House of Atreus, the self-wrought tragedy of Oedipus, even *la crise psychologique* of the *Bacchae*: it is no less than the cry, muted, parabolic, ironical, but nonetheless genuine and impassioned, despairing the destruction, both spiritual and moral, of Athens herself. *Helen* is not a tragedy: but behind it lies one of civilization's greatest tragedies. Once this is understood, much else falls into place, and the depth of the underlying philosophical themes discerned by Charles Segal becomes comprehensible in a way that would hardly be the case in the light-hearted frolic postulated by Webster. And—a woman's play? Yes, certainly. It is not women who make war. The men in *Helen* are all warriors, of a kind, and poorly do they come out of it; but for morality, justice, compassion (a quality of extreme rarity in Greek tragedy) we must go to Helen and Theonöe. No need for Verrall's elaborate hypothesis when a much more plausible explanation lies before our very eyes.

Aristophanes, of course, did much the same sort of thing, but in a less constricted medium (and with a correspondingly greater risk of prosecution). As we have already observed, his acute ear and eyes were to make practical use of *Helen* in the *Thesmophoriazusae* in 411 B.C.; but he had already written and produced his own version of *Helen—The Birds—*in 414 B.C., not long after the Sicilian Expedition had set sail (and well before any authoritative report of success or failure could have reached Athens). *Birds* is a play of escape—*the* play of escape: where after all was Cloud-Cuckoo-Land invented? A play does not need to drive lessons home in a heavy-handed manner to be effective. Euripides, like Aristophanes, was unusually lucky in his audiences.

It remains to place *Helen* within the broader sweep of Athenian history. Close in time to *Lysistrata* (another play, interestingly enough, in which anti-Laconian feelings are muted), it must have held a poignant message for Athenians who had already been at war for nearly twenty years and who were still to be at war for another eight. With the benefit of hindsight, we can see that the great years of Athens, in both physical and cultural terms, were approaching their end. Sophocles and Euripides were both to die before the turn of the century; Aristophanes' verve would soon vanish, to decline into the duller ore of the *Ploutos*. The age of Pericles had already been replaced by men of lesser stamp— Cleon, Theramenes, and the like. For Athens, the fifth century B.C. was a glorious one, but it took an appalling toll: one thinks of the famous inscription, now in the Louvre, commemorating those of the Erechtheid tribe who died, all in the same year, fighting "in Cyprus, in Egypt, in Phoenicia, at Halieis, in Aegina, at Megara." The year was 459 B.C., just before the production of *Eumenides*. Just before the outbreak of the Peloponnesian War, in the spring of 431 B.C., Euripides himself breathed the spirit of Periclean optimism in a chorus of the *Medea*:

From old the sons of Erechtheus know felicity;
The children of blessed gods,
Born from a land holy and undespoiled,
They pasture on glorious wisdom
Ever walking gracefully through the brightest of skies,
Where once, men tell, the Holy Nine,
The Pierian Muses,
Created golden-haired Harmony.
(TR. C. M. BOWRA)

In 430, Euripides produced his *Children of Herakles*, presenting in an heroic setting an ideal Athens which assumes responsibility for the oppressed, whencesoever they come. In 424, in the *Suppliants*, Athens is still an ideal city, a true democracy, the home of free speech. But Pericles died in 429 B.C., and Euripides lived on to produce *Helen*, in which a glittering façade of point and counterpoint does so much to conceal "something far more deeply interfused": the futility of war, the especial futility and immorality of *this* war, and the inexorable decline of Athens.

THE TEXT

We have normally, but not invariably, followed the text favored by A. M. Dale in her edition (Oxford, 1967). The text of *Helen* has come down to us in a very imperfect state (it is one of those nine plays of Euripides for which there is only a single manuscript tradition) and in places it is seriously, even desperately, corrupt; this is especially the case in the choruses (where copyists were always apt to become confused owing to their ignorance of the meters employed and the difficulty of the language) where, all too often, one can do little better than follow what was probably the intended sense. It is difficult to overestimate the importance of this—and the difficulties which are thereby posed for the translator. In an exegetical edition one can discuss textual cruces, point out the problems, arrive at a preferred solution—or decide that one cannot be found. The translator has no such resource; and we can do no more than to indicate in the notes a few of those places where the text is most deeply corrupted and what an alternative rendering might be. More than this: there are places where we do not know, and cannot know, for certain, who is speaking (there are several such places in *Helen*, one of them of great importance). Actors' later interpolations, too, abound, and we have taken a sturdy approach: when we believe—usually in concert with A. M. Dale—that lines have been interpolated, we have omitted them. It should be added that such lines often give themselves away by their awkwardness, extravagance, or irrelevance. In reading a translation, it is only natural for the Greekless reader to assume that the text has been transmitted straight from heaven; we ask you to remember that such is very far from being the case. Our own faith has by no means always proved robust enough to feel really confident that Euripides wrote such-and-such and not anything else in any given passage; but translators must wield swords to cut the most Gordian of knots.

The foregoing comments refer to, but do little to describe, the remarkable thesis advanced by A. W. Verrall (*Four Plays of Euripides*, Cambridge University Press, 1905, pp. 43-133). Verrall was famous for providing a perverse answer to the right question, and it is worthwhile looking briefly at what he says on *Helen*, not because of his far-fetched solution, but because of the questions which he, explicitly or implicitly, raises. Verrall argues that *Helen* was originally not written for public presentation, but as an ironic and partly self-parodying drama, composed for private performance at a house on the island of Helenē belonging to a woman of Athens, the occasion being a gathering of women who had been celebrating the Thesmophoria. Needless to rehearse Verrall's arguments; what are the reasons which have led him to theorize in this way? Just those odd aspects of the play to which we have drawn attention:

A. the rehabilitation of Helen, least reputable of her sex;
B. the seeming irrelevance of the "Great Mother" choric ode;
C. the strangely unused omniscience of Theonöe;
D. certain structural parallels with *Iphigeneia in Tauris*;
E. the superfluity of the Teucer episode.

And there are other points, sometimes (to be candid) of an implausibly detailed nature. Here we need only observe that Verrall's acute eye, striking at an angle to reality, has observed just those anomalies which have led us to a quite different, perhaps more mundane, conclusion. But in one, relatively minor, point, Verrall's analysis is faultless. Menelaos is generally, as already noted, really rather stupid. But at one point, when Helen proposes that he should pretend to be the reporter of his own death, he retorts: "But how will this trick help our combined escape?/ It's rather an old-fashioned one, you know." (1131-32). Yes, indeed: both Aeschylus (in *Choephori*) and Sophocles (in *Electra*) had used the device before, and it is just that fact that, very boldly, he is referring to. A line like that serves to remind us that there was an ironic as well as a deeper side to the *Helen*; a flawed jewel, but a jewel.

Oxford, England   COLIN LEACH

HELEN

CHARACTERS

HELEN daughter of Zeus and Leda

TEUCER a Greek

CHORUS of captive Spartan women

LEADER

MENELAOS husband of Helen and King of Sparta

OLD WOMAN portress at the palace

SERVANT one of Menelaos's men

THEONÖE sister of Theoklymenos

THEOKLYMENOS King of Egypt

MESSENGER a servant of Theoklymenos

DIOSKOUROI KASTOR AND POLYDEUKES, sons of Zeus and Leda, now gods

Line numbers in the right-hand margin refer to the English translation only, and the Notes at p. 87 are keyed to these lines. The bracketed line numbers in the running headlines refer to the Greek text.

The scene is Egypt, before the royal palace. On one side of the stage is the tomb of King Proteus, where HELEN has taken sanctuary.

The stage represents a palace front, with central double doors. To the left of the stage is the substantial structure of the tomb of Proteus, King of Egypt. HELEN is found center-stage.

HELEN Here live the lovely water-nymphs of Nile
who brings the melted white snow down to water
the plains of Egypt starved of blesséd rain.
Proteus was king here, when he lived, controlling
all Egypt from his island home of Pharos.
He'd married one of the sea-nymphs, Psamathe,
who'd left her husband Aiakos, and she bore him
two children in this palace: first a son,
Theoklymenos, and then a young princess,
the apple of her mother's eye—Eido   10
she was named as a child, but when she reached the age
of marriage she was called Theonöe,
for she had understanding of all things
that are, and are to come, prophetic powers
inherited from her mother's father, Nereus.
My own home country, though, is pretty well known,
for it's Sparta, and my father was Tyndareus.
There's an old story that Zeus changed himself
into a swan once and, being chased by an eagle,
flew to my mother Leda's lap for refuge   20
and by that trick got what he wanted from her—
which may or may not be true. My name is Helen.
Now let me tell you my sad history.
The three goddesses, Hera, Aphrodite,
and Zeus-born, virgin Athene, went one day
to Paris's valley hide-out on Mount Ida
quarreling about their beauty and determined
to have the issue judged. And Aphrodite

offered my beauty—if anything can be called
beautiful that brings misery—as a bribe,   30
and me as a wife, to Paris, and so won.
Paris quitted his mountain herds and came
to Sparta to collect his bride; but then
Hera, disgruntled in defeat, deprived
her rival's solid promise of all substance:
she gave the Trojan prince not the real me
but a living likeness conjured out of air,
so that believing he possesses me
he possesses only his belief. Then Zeus
compounded these misfortunes with new plans,   40
for in order to relieve the cumbered earth
of her plethora of children and to enhance
the reputation of the mightiest Greek
he loaded with a war the land of Greece
and the unlucky Phrygians. Yet all those years
the Helen who endured the siege of Troy,
the Helen the Greek spears fought for as a prize,
was me only in name. For I myself
was wrapped in a cloud, hurried through pockets of air
and set down in the palace of Proteus here   50
by Hermes—proof that Zeus did not forget me;
indeed he chose the most civilized of men
to help me keep my marriage-bed unstained.
So here I've been while my unhappy husband,
bent on recovering me, mustered an army
and sailed off to the battlements of Troy.
Men died for me in thousands by Skamander,
and I, the passive sufferer in it all,
became anathema, for it seemed to the world
that I had betrayed my husband and that he   60
had pushed Greece into a disastrous war.
Then why do I go on living? For this reason:
I have it on the authority of Hermes
that once my husband learns the truth—that never
did I go to Troy, never was I unfaithful—
I shall live with him again in famous Sparta.

HELEN *moves left across stage to stand by the tomb of*
Proteus.

As long as the old king Proteus enjoyed life
I was immune from suitors, but his son,
Theoklymenos, now that he's dead and buried,
haunts me and hunts me—which is why I've come,   70
loyal to my vows to Menelaos,
to the tomb of Proteus as a suppliant
to pray for their preservation. Thus at least,
although my name is vilified through Greece,
my body here remains free from reproach.

Enter TEUCER, *right. He first sees and is impressed by*
the imposing form of the palace, then, almost at once,
catches sight of HELEN.

TEUCER Who is the lord of this imposing place?
These royal precincts, this proud corniced mass,
suggest the house of the God of Wealth himself.
Hah!
Ye gods, what's this I see? An abomination!   80
The very image of that murderous woman
who was the ruin of me and all the Greeks!
May the gods abhor you for resembling Helen!
If I weren't a guest standing on foreign soil
one of my trusty arrows would soon pay you
for looking like the daughter of Zeus—with death.

HELEN Poor man, whoever you are, don't flinch away.
Why detest *me* because of what happened to *her?*

TEUCER My fault—my anger got the better of me,
for the whole of Greece loathes the daughter of Zeus.   90
Forgive me, lady, for the words I spoke.

HELEN Who are you, though? Whereabouts do you come from?

TEUCER I am one of the Greeks who fought and suffered.

HELEN   No wonder, then, that you abominate Helen.

TEUCER   My name is Teucer, Telamon was my father,
        and I was born and raised in Salamis.

HELEN   What brings you, then, to the delta of the Nile?

TEUCER   I am an exile. I was driven from home.

HELEN   You have my sympathy. Who was responsible?

TEUCER   The closest friend a man could have—my father!   100

HELEN   But why? For the fact implies some sort of doom.

TEUCER   My brother Ajax died at Troy—my doom.

HELEN   How? You didn't kill him yourself, surely?

TEUCER   He died by his own hand, fell on his sword.

HELEN   Was he mad, then? No one sane attempts self-slaughter.

TEUCER   Have you heard of a certain Achilles, Peleus' son?

HELEN   He was one of Helen's suitors, I've been told.

TEUCER   When he died he left his arms to be contested.

HELEN   And how could that have caused Ajax's death?

TEUCER   Another man won the arms—and he killed himself.   110

HELEN   And so your troubles stem direct from his?

TEUCER   They do, in that I failed to die with him.

HELEN   Did you really go to the famous city of Troy?

TEUCER I brought about its downfall—and my own.

HELEN And is it razed flat now, burnt to the ground?

TEUCER So thoroughly that no trace of a wall is left.

HELEN Oh, Helen, Helen, for you the Trojans perished!

TEUCER The Trojans? The Greeks too! A holocaust!

HELEN How long is it since the city was destroyed?

TEUCER Almost seven harvests have gone round since then.   120

HELEN And before that how long were you at Troy?

TEUCER Innumerable months, ten years in all.

HELEN Tell me, did you capture the Spartan woman?

TEUCER Menelaos did, and dragged her off by the hair.

HELEN Did you see the unhappy queen? Or is this hearsay?

TEUCER I saw her as plainly as I'm seeing you.

HELEN But perhaps the gods made you imagine it all.

TEUCER Please talk of something else. Stop harping on her.

HELEN And is Menelaos home now with his wife?

TEUCER He's certainly not in Argos—nor in Sparta.   130

HELEN That's terrible news—for some who hear it anyway.

TEUCER He's said to have vanished, lost, and his wife with him.

HELEN But surely all the Greeks sailed back together?

TEUCER They did, but a storm scattered them far apart.

HELEN Where were they on the wide salt sea when it struck?

TEUCER Halfway through their passage of the Aegean.

HELEN And no one's had news since of his having landed?

TEUCER No one. All Greece considers him as dead.

HELEN (aside) I am crushed. (To TEUCER) And Thestios'
        daughter—is she living?

TEUCER Leda, you mean? No, she died long ago.   140

HELEN You're not suggesting Helen's disgrace destroyed her?

TEUCER They say so. Though she was royal, she hanged herself.

HELEN And her sons, Kastor, Polydeukes—dead or alive?

TEUCER Both, you might say. There are two different rumors.

HELEN Give me the stronger one. (Aside) Nothing but grief!

TEUCER It's said they became gods, in the shape of stars.

HELEN Those words are welcome, but what's the other story?

TEUCER That shame for their sister made them end their lives
        on their own swords. But enough of tales of the past—
        I've no desire for a second bout of tears.   150
        My reason for arriving at this palace
        is to see the prophetess Theonöe.
        Will you introduce me, so that I can ask
        advice from the oracle how best to obtain
        a fair wind for my voyage on to Cyprus?
        For Apollo has told me I shall settle there

and give the island name of Salamis
to my new home in memory of my birthplace.

HELEN The ship and the sea will guide you there themselves.
But, sir, make your getaway from this place   160
before Theoklymenos sees you—he's the king:
at the moment he's away, bloodily engaged
in slaughtering animals with his pack of hounds—
for any Greek caught here he puts to death.
Don't press me to know why, I'm saying nothing;
and anyway what good could the knowledge do you?

TEUCER Kind and frank words, which I appreciate, lady.
May the gods reward you richly in return!
Your similarity to Helen is only
skin-deep; inside you're not a bit like her.   170
May she die horribly and never reach home,
but you—good luck be with you all your life!

Exit TEUCER *right. The* CHORUS *of captive Greek women*
enters left.

HELEN Raising a great cry for a great grief,
how shall I bring my misery to birth
for its relief?
To what spirit of music shall I appeal
for a dirge, for a lament
bitter enough to suit
the burden of sorrow I feel?
Come, deathly daughters of Earth,   180
you sirens with bird-wings,
and with your pipe or lyre or Libyan flute
strike up a sad accompaniment,
some grim, despairing strain
in sympathy with my sufferings,
in harmony with my pain,
so that your music, matching my agony,
may as my offering please Persephone

down in her dark hall—
a chant of blood, a black paean rising in unison   190
with the tears I now let fall
for the souls of the dead and gone.

Enter CHORUS

CHORUS By the blue pool, where the young rushes throng,
        I happened to be drying
        in the sun's golden beams
        my purple clothing spread
        on the curling grass's bed
        when I heard a pitiful crying,
        no voice of joy, no song
        fit for the lyre, but anguished, haunting screams   200
        such as a mountain nymph, a naiad, flying
        from Pan's brute force
        might utter, at bay, in the rocky hollow of her source.

HELEN   Women of Greece, captives of a foreign oar,
        I have news for your ears.
        A Greek mariner has come ashore
        bringing fresh tears to mingle with my tears.
        Troy is a smoking ruin of war,
        destroyed by my deadly face—
        or, rather, by my ill-used name.   210
        Leda, my mother,
        has put a noose round her neck for shame
        of my disgrace.
        My wandering, sea-tossed
        husband is lost, is lost,
        and Sparta's glory and pride,
        Kastor and his twin-born brother,
        will never, never be seen again
        on the pounded, hoof-ringing plain
        or the meadows beside   220
        reed-fringed Eurotas where the young men used to
            train—
        wrestle and run and ride.

CHORUS Mourn, mourn
        for Helen hounded by her doom.
        Lady, you were given
        a mocking gift, a life not to be borne,
        when Zeus swooped from mid-heaven
        in the shape of a swan
        and with a flash of snow-white wings
        planted you in your mother's womb.   230
        Since then what sufferings,
        what trials have you not undergone?
        Leda is dead;
        your two brothers, the beloved sons
        of Zeus, are far away from happiness;
        your land of birth is hidden from your eyes;
        throughout the cities of Greece there runs
        a rumor, lady, that implies
        you sleep in a barbarian's embrace;
        your lord is a corpse on the sea's bed;   240
        never again will you bless
        your father's house or grace
        Athene's brazen temple with your face.

HELEN   Alas, whose hand in the known world felled
        the pine that ultimately spelled
        ruin to Troy? For from that tree was nailed
        and hammered the ship that Paris sailed
        with his pirate oarsmen over the waves
        to shatter the peace
        of my hearth in his quest for the prize   250
        of my lovely disastrous eyes
        and the pleasures of my marriage-bed;
        and with him, false to all she'd said,
        came the murderous goddess of love who sent to their
            graves
        the warriors of both Troy and Greece.
        And then her highness Hera,
        who shares the bed of Zeus and on a gold throne
        sits beside him, sent her message-bearer,
        the swift-footed son of Maia, down.

He caught me   260
when I was gathering fresh roses in my gown
to take to Athene's temple, snatched me and brought me
through the glittering zone
of air to this bleak shore,
where I became
a wretched prize in the fierce tug of war
between all Greece and Priam's sons.
And now, where the river Simois runs,
I'm soiled with a false shame
that's mine only in name, only in name.   270

LEADER You have sorrow enough, we know; but one must bear
the burdens of life as lightly as one can.

HELEN Look at me, friends. I'm yoked, half-choked with
            trouble!
Was I not born a monster? My entire life,
every wretched event, has been unnatural,
for which I blame my beauty as much as Hera.
If only it could have been wiped clean like a picture
and something less alluring painted over,
so that the Greeks, forgetting the blemishes
that chance has put on me, might bear in mind   280
my better, not my worse side, as they do.
When a person's hopes hang on a single issue
and the gods treat him badly, then it's hard,
but still it's bearable. But in my case
misfortunes hem me in from all directions.
In the first place, I'm both innocent *and* slandered—
and being saddled with another's crimes
cuts deeper than the burden of your own.
On top of that the gods uprooted me
from my own fatherland and put me down   290
here, among savages, cut off from friends,
a slave among slaves, for in barbarian countries
all men in effect are slaves except for one.
And the sole anchor in my sea of troubles,

the hope that my husband would arrive one day
and rescue me, is gone, for he's gone too—
dead. And my mother's dead, and I "destroyed" her—
untrue, unjust, but the injustice sticks.
My daughter, once the sunshine of my life
and all our house, withers in spinsterhood,   300
dead are my two twin brothers whom they call
the sons of Zeus, and dead is my own heart
through what's been done to me, though I live on.
And last and worst, even if I did reach home
they'd bar the gates, thinking I was the Helen
that Menelaos went to fetch from Troy.
If my husband were alive, he'd recognize me,
as I should him, by certain special signs
private to us; but he's not, he's lost forever.
Then why am I still alive? What's left to suffer?   310
I could choose marriage as a way of escape,
live with this uncouth foreigner and preside
at his rich table, but when a husband's hateful
to a wife she hates even the richest house.
This is the doom and depth of my despair:
the very beauty that makes other women
happy has proved for me a blasting curse.

LEADER Helen, don't be too sure that what that Greek,
        whoever he is, reported is all true.

HELEN But he made it clear enough my husband's dead.   320

LEADER The spoken word can often turn out false.

HELEN But equally it can have the ring of truth.

LEADER You're biased towards the dark view, not the bright.

HELEN It's fear that grips and drives me—into fear.

LEADER How much goodwill do you have inside the palace?

HELEN They're all my friends, except my hot pursuer.

LEADER Do you know what you must do now? Leave this
             sanctuary—

HELEN What are you trying to say? What's your proposal?

LEADER —and go to the house of the daughter of the sea,
             the Nereid Theonöe, who knows all things.   330
             Ask *her* whether your husband's still alive,
             enjoying daylight. When you've got your answer,
             weep or rejoice according to the news;
             for what good can it do you to grieve now,
             before you know the facts? Listen to me.
             I'm willing to accompany you myself
             to ask for her clairvoyant revelation.
             Women should always give each other help.

HELEN Friends, I shall do what you say.
             Hurry to the palace, hurry through the gate   340
             to learn the outcome of my fate.

CHORUS You call me; gladly I go.

HELEN Ai, ai, black day!
             What words of horror or unhappiness
             am I about to hear?

CHORUS Dear heart, don't leap ahead of your fear,
             don't play the prophetess
             to your own woe.

HELEN What deep distress
             has my husband suffered? Does he see the sun   350
             chariot his four horses
             and the stars run
             on their nightly courses,
             or does he share the dead man's doom below?

CHORUS   Accept the future, whatever
        face it may wear, as a friend.

HELEN   Eurotas, my home river,
        sweet-running and reed-green,
        to you I appeal,
        be my witness: if the report is true   360
        that my husband's dead, I swear I shall end—

CHORUS   What do these wild words mean?

HELEN   I shall pay the price
        of my guilt with my life—
        noose my neck with a strangling rope
        or use the bloody, throat-severing knife
        till the sharp, cold thrust of steel
        and the flesh's cruel ordeal
        make of my death a sacrifice
        to the three goddesses and Priam's boy,   370
        who once kept herds and tuned his pipe on Ida's slope.

CHORUS   May bad luck shift elsewhere and leave you hope.

HELEN   Oh, suffering, pitiful Troy,
        destroyed by a deed of mine that was never done!
        My beauty, Aphrodite's gift, which won
        the prize, has borne a monstrous child
        of blood and tears, agony piled
        on agony, sorrow multiplied
        on sorrow. Countless mothers mourn a son,
        and countless Trojan girls,   380
        sisters of corpses, have shaved off their curls
        in grief by swirling Skamander's side.
        Greece, too, wails
        inconsolably for her Greeks;
        a river of tears runs for her dead;
        she has beaten her fists against her head
        and scored her fingernails
        in stripes across her cheeks

till the soft skin bled.
Happy Arcadian girl, who long ago   390
shared Zeus's bed,
Kallisto—you relieved your weight of woe
when you were transformed to a bear
with rough pelt and paws and savage glare—
punishment lighter than my mother earned.
Happy, too, daughter of Merops, Titan maid,
whom Artemis in the days of old
expelled from her chaste company—you paid
your beauty's penalty by being turned
into a hind with horns of gold.   400
But *mine* has burned, has burned
Troy's citadel
and been the death of my own Greeks as well.

HELEN *and the* CHORUS *exeunt center through the double
doors of the palace, in order to consult* THEONÖE. MENE-
LAOS *enters right; he is in rags and presents a woebegone
appearance, having come from the seacoast.*

MENELAOS O grandfather Pelops, who at Pisa once
won the great chariot-race with Oinomaos,
would that your life had ended the same day
you were served up as a banquet for the gods!
Instead, revived by them, you lived to father
Atreus, who in his turn, with Aerope,
produced that famous couple, Agamemnon   410
and myself, Menelaos. I consider—
and I don't say this to boast—that of the Greeks
I shipped the largest expeditionary force
to Troy—and my authority as king
owed nothing to compulsion, being based
on willing obedience from the men I led.
The count of those who died and those who escaped
the perils of the sea and got back safely
with the names of all the dead can now be reckoned
exactly. I'm the exception, for ever since   420

I sacked the towers of Troy I've been a miserable
wanderer on the grey-green, rolling seas,
longing for my own country, which, it seems,
the gods think me unworthy to rejoin.
I've sailed to every lonely landing-place
and hostile port in Libya; every time
I near my native shore gales beat me back;
not once have I had the wind I need for home.
And now I'm here, a wretched castaway—
my comrades lost, our ship split on the rocks   430
and smashed to flotsam—washed up on this coast.
I found a floating keel, all that was left,
on which in my desperate danger with great difficulty
I got to land, saving Helen as well,
my prize from Troy. Who the inhabitants are
or what this place is called I've no idea.
Out of embarrassment I avoided the crowd
and so never asked, concealing my distress,
ashamed at my shabby state, for when a man
of high importance falls on evil times   440
he feels it more than one inured to hardship
because it's unfamiliar. I'm in fact
at the end of my tether—no food, and no clothes
to cover me—as anyone can tell,
what I'm wearing are torn sails saved from the wreck,
for the sea has confiscated my magnificent,
luxurious wardrobe. Meanwhile, having hidden
the cause of all my sufferings, my wife,
in the depths of a cave and charged my fellow-survivors
with the task of guarding her, I've come on my own   450
to try and scrounge provisions for my shipmates.
When I saw these high, topped walls and the grand gates
I thought, "Some rich man's mansion," and approached,
since there's always hope in the houses of the wealthy
for sailors in need; from the poor they can't get help,
even though the will to give it may be there.
Hallo, there! Is there a porter around to take
the news of my predicament inside?

MENELAOS *has been moving toward the palace doors*
during the last lines of his speech. As he knocks, an OLD
WOMAN, *the portress, appears at the doors; she is both*
busy and irritable.

OLD WOMAN   Who's this at the door? Be off with you at once!
Stop hanging about the porch and bothering
my lords and masters—or you'll end up dead,
for you look like a Greek, and we've no truck with
Greeks.

460

MENELAOS   Well said, old lady! A fine speech! All right,
I'll behave myself. Only less temper, please.

OLD WOMAN   Be off, I tell you. Stranger, I've strict orders
not to allow any Greek inside the house.

The OLD WOMAN *moves threateningly toward* MENELAOS.

MENELAOS   Look here, don't wave your arms and jostle me!

OLD WOMAN   It's your fault for not doing what I say.

MENELAOS   Go in and announce to your master that I'm here.

OLD WOMAN   I won't be at all popular if I do.

470

MENELAOS   As a shipwrecked foreigner I'm a protected person.

OLD WOMAN   Off with you now and try another house.

MENELAOS *speaks blusteringly.*

MENELAOS   I shan't. I'm coming in. Do as I order.

OLD WOMAN   You're being a nuisance, you know. You'll get thrown
out.

MENELAOS   Ah, where's my famous army now? I need it!

OLD WOMAN You may have been someone elsewhere; here you're
             nobody.

MENELAOS My soul, do we deserve this? What an insult!

OLD WOMAN Tears in your eyes, eh? Who are you moaning to?

MENELAOS Only the happy days I used to know.

OLD WOMAN Then go and dump your tears on your old friends.   480

MENELAOS What country am I in? Whose palace is this?

                        The OLD WOMAN *points to Proteus' tomb.*

OLD WOMAN This is the house of Proteus. You're in Egypt.

MENELAOS Egypt? So it's an ill wind blew me here!

OLD WOMAN What have you got against our shining Nile?

MENELAOS Nothing at all. It's my own luck I'm cursing.

OLD WOMAN Plenty of folk have troubles—you're not the first.

MENELAOS Your king, whatever you call him—is he at home?

OLD WOMAN This tomb you see is his. His son reigns now.

MENELAOS Then where *is* he? Inside the house, or away?

OLD WOMAN Not at home. And he's a hater of all Greeks.   490

MENELAOS To what do I owe this dubious benefit?

OLD WOMAN Helen, the daughter of Zeus, is here in the palace.

MENELAOS What? Did I hear you rightly? Say that again.

OLD WOMAN Tyndareus' daughter, the one who lived in Sparta.

MENELAOS Where did she come from? What's the explanation?

OLD WOMAN From Sparta of course—from *her* country to ours.

MENELAOS But when? (*Aside*): Surely not captured from the cave?

OLD WOMAN Before the Greeks went off to Troy, my friend.
But make yourself scarce, for things inside the palace
have taken a most upsetting turn just now.   500
You've come at a bad time. If my royal master
catches you here, your welcome will be death.
I'm a friend of the Greeks more than my words let on:
if I spoke harshly, it was for fear of *him*.

Exit OLD WOMAN *into the palace.* MENELAOS *soliloquizes.*

MENELAOS I'm at a loss. What am I to think? She tells me
of new disasters following in the train
of the old ones. If I really seized my wife
in Troy and brought her here with me and put her
under guard in a cave, it must be another woman
bearing the same name who's in the house.   510
She called her the daughter of Zeus. Is there a *man*
by the name of Zeus living beside the Nile?
No, for there's one Zeus only—the one in heaven.
And where else in the world can there be a Sparta
except beside the reed-bright, rippling Eurotas?
Tyndareus is a unique and well-known name.
Can there possibly be a second Sparta *and*
another Troy? I don't know what to make of it.
But the earth's a big place, I suppose—many things
must share one name, cities and women too;   520
there's nothing strange in that. And I refuse
to be frightened off by the barking of a servant.
No man alive could be so uncivilized
as to deny me food, especially having

learnt who I am, for the fires of Troy are famous
and so is the man who lit them—Menelaos,
a name that's recognized throughout the world.
I shall wait here for the master of the house.
He poses me two choices: if he's savage,
I'll hide, then make my way back to the wreck;   530
if he shows signs of tenderheartedness,
I'll ask for supplies to meet our needs. This, then,
was the ultimate indignity for me—
that I, a king myself, should have to beg
food from my fellow-kings to stay alive.
Still, what must be must be. It was a wise
philosopher, not I, who coined the phrase,
"Nothing's as strong as brute necessity."

> The CHORUS re-enters center; MENELAOS remains on
> stage, partly concealed by the tomb of Proteus.

CHORUS Within the palace we have heard
the virgin prophetess speak. Her word   540
was unambiguous: she said
that Menelaos has not gone to his grave,
to the darkly glimmering cavern of the dead,
but has been a wanderer, hard-driven
over the heaving wave,
since he left Troy with his splashing oar,
never anchoring in his native haven
and skirting every shore
from here to the world's ends,
miserable, hungry, friendless, far from friends.   550

> Re-enter HELEN center; she begins to move toward the
> sanctuary of the tomb.

HELEN Now back to my station at the sanctuary,
having heard Theonöe's welcome revelation.
She knows the truth of all things, and she says
that my husband is alive, lives, sees the daylight,

that having weathered countless passages,
no novice in the school of travel, and after
wandering about the world, he'll find at last
the appointed end of all his sufferings—here.
One thing she didn't mention: when he arrives,
will he be spared? For, overjoyed at hearing   560
that he lived, I failed to press home the question.
She also said that he's escaped a shipwreck
with a few friends and at this very moment
is somewhere near. Dear husband, when will you come?
And if you come what a void in my heart you'll fill!

HELEN *catches sight of the crouching, semi-hidden*
MENELAOS *and at once hurries to the tomb. Until line*
              591 she adopts an attitude of extreme caution.

Help! Who's this man? Is this a plot, some ambush
laid by the sacrilegious son of Proteus?
Quick as a racehorse or a bacchanal
to the tomb, with flying feet! He looks so savage
I think he means to hunt me down for prey.   570

MENELAOS Stop! Why this desperate, frantic struggle to reach
the floor and smoke-warmed pillars of the tomb?
Don't run away. When you revealed your face
it struck me speechless with astonishment.

HELEN Friends, I am being outraged. This man is barring
my way to sanctuary. He wants to seize me
and force me to accept the king's embrace.

MENELAOS I'm not a bandit or a hired abductor.

HELEN The clothes you're wearing, though, are ugly enough.

MENELAOS Stand still. Stop darting away. Don't be afraid.   580

HELEN Very well, I'll stand here, now I've reached the tomb.

MENELAOS Lady, who are you? Whose face am I looking at?

HELEN And who are you? Our questions are the same.

MENELAOS I never in my life saw such a resemblance—

HELEN You gods! For recognition *is* a god—

MENELAOS Are you a Greek or a native of this country?

HELEN A Greek. And you? I long to know as well.

MENELAOS Lady, you look uncannily like Helen.

HELEN And you like Menelaos. What does it mean?

MENELAOS The truth. I am that most unhappy man.   590

HELEN O long-lost husband, come to your wife's arms!

MENELAOS What do you mean—wife? Don't finger my clothes.

HELEN The wife that Tyndareus, my father, gave you.

MENELAOS Torch-bearing Hekate, send me kinder visions!

HELEN I am no moonlight ghost of the crossways goddess.

MENELAOS No more than I am the husband of two women.

HELEN Who is this other woman whose lord you are?

MENELAOS The wife I brought from Troy and hid in the cave.

HELEN I am your wife; you have no other queen.

MENELAOS My mind is clear enough—but are my eyes?   600

HELEN Yes; for surely you recognize your wife?

MENELAOS You look like her, indeed I won't deny it.

HELEN Whom should you trust for proof if not your eyes?

MENELAOS They fail me here: I have another wife.

HELEN But I never went to Troy. That was a phantom.

MENELAOS Come, who on earth can make a living likeness?

HELEN She was formed of air by the gods, to be your bride.

MENELAOS And which god modeled her? It's past belief.

HELEN Hera—in order to palm her off on Paris.

MENELAOS You were here, then, *and* in Troy, at the same time?   610

HELEN A name can travel where a body can't.

MENELAOS Let me alone. I'd troubles enough before.

HELEN Will you leave me, then, to go with your shadow-wife?

MENELAOS Yes, it's farewell. Good luck, since you're like Helen.

HELEN Those words destroy me. A husband found—and lost!

MENELAOS The pain I felt at Troy outweighs your talk.

HELEN Alas, was ever woman so unhappy?
My dearest ones desert me; now I'll never
find my way back to Greece and home again.

> *Enter a* MESSENGER *right, one of* MENELAOS' *senior
> henchmen. He is agitated and out of breath; he
> intercepts* MENELAOS.

SERVANT   Menelaos! I've been wandering all over   620
          this barbarous country looking for you, sent
          by the men you left. Finding you's been hard work.

MENELAOS What's happened? The foreigners haven't robbed you,
              have they?

SERVANT   A weird thing. But words pale beside the fact.

MENELAOS Go on. This urgency must mean strange news.

SERVANT   The hardships you endured were all for nothing!

MENELAOS You're harping on old sorrows. What's new, though?

SERVANT   Your wife's gone. She vanished, she was spirited
          out of the special cave which we were guarding
          into the folds of the air, some hiding-place   630
          in the sky. Before she went, she just said this:
          "O poor, long-suffering Trojans and all you Greeks
          who fought at Troy, it was because of me
          that you died on Skamander's banks, as Hera planned,
          imagining Paris had Helen in his bed,
          when he never did. The time's arrived for me,
          having done my duty here as Fate ordained,
          to return to my father, the sky. I pity Helen,
          daughter of Tyndareus, who's heard her name
          baselessly slandered though she's innocent."   640

              He sees HELEN *and continues rather crossly.*

          Greetings, daughter of Leda. So you've been *here?*
          I've just reported that you'd disappeared
          into starry space, being quite unaware
          that you'd sprouted wings. Next time I shan't allow you
          to fool us with another trick like this:
          you gave your husband and his followers
          more than their fill of trouble over in Troy.

43

MENELAOS At last the answer! It all fits together—
          what she said was true. O dearly longed-for day
          that brings you to my arms, my close embrace.   650

          MENELAOS *embraces* HELEN; *the* SERVANT *looks on in*
                                                    surprise.

HELEN   Menelaos, dearest of men,
          our time of waiting has grown grey and old,
          but our joy now is fresh and bright.
          Women, I have my husband again
          to cherish and to hold.
          After long wheelings of the sun,
          bringer of daily light,
          in a rapture I clasp my beloved one.

MENELAOS And I've found you. Since we have been apart
          there's so much to tell between us, where shall I start?   660

HELEN   For joy the hairs on my head
          rise and shiver, for joy I shed
          tears, and for joy I wind
          my arms round your body fast,
          happy, O dearest husband, happy at last.

MENELAOS O precious face, I have no fault to find:
          the daughter of Zeus' and Leda's bed
          is mine again, is mine—
          she whom the twin brothers who ride
          white horses brought me as a bride   670
          with double blessings under the shine
          of torches on that long-ago day.
          And now the god who stole you away
          from me and my house is leading us on
          to better things, and the dark times are gone.

HELEN   Lucky misfortune, husband, has brought us together
          after a long, long storm; but now that it's fair
          I pray to enjoy the weather.

MENELAOS May you enjoy it—I repeat your prayer.
　　　　　With two like us, who must share,   680
　　　　　joy and sorrow cannot be separated.

　　HELEN Dear, good friends, I no longer regret
　　　　　the past or begrudge its misery.
　　　　　I have my husband, he belongs to me
　　　　　after the many years I waited—oh, how I waited
　　　　　for him to return from Troy!

MENELAOS I am yours, you are mine:
　　　　　we have each other again.
　　　　　Having watched thousands of sad suns set
　　　　　in my delusion, only now can I guess   690
　　　　　Hera's design.
　　　　　But now my tears are of joy,
　　　　　now I have far more happiness
　　　　　than ever I had pain.

　　HELEN What can I say?
　　　　　Who could have ever hoped
　　　　　for such unhoped-for bliss—
　　　　　to hold you in my arms like this!

MENELAOS As I hold you—you who I thought had eloped
　　　　　to the city of Ida, those grim, doomed towers.   700
　　　　　Tell me, by all the holy powers,
　　　　　how did you steal from my house that day?

　　HELEN A cruel question which gives me pause:
　　　　　you probe cruelly back to the first cause.

MENELAOS Tell me, for what the gods on high
　　　　　give we must hear and bear below.

　　HELEN I spit away the words I have to speak.

MENELAOS But speak you must;
　　　　　for my sake try—
　　　　　there's pleasure in hearing of an ancient woe.   710

45

HELEN I never ran away to seek
       that foreign prince's bed of shame,
       hurried away by oars, carried away by lust.

MENELAOS What god or power, though, bore you like a prize
          from your own land?

HELEN Husband, it was the son of Zeus, Hermes, who came,
       decoyed me
       and brought me to the Nile.

MENELAOS Incredible! At whose command?
          This is a tale too wild to understand.   720

HELEN I have wept and wept, and my eyes
       are wet with tears still. The wife of Zeus destroyed me.

MENELAOS Hera? But why should she bear us spite?

HELEN Alas, the source of my sufferings
       was Ida's source—the bathing springs
       where the three goddesses washed their bodies bright
       and beauty came to trial.

MENELAOS And why did the trial make Hera work you ill?

HELEN Why? She robbed Paris of . . . MENELAOS Of what?

HELEN Of me, whom Aphrodite had guaranteed   730
       as his future bride.

MENELAOS Cruel goddess! HELEN Cruel indeed!
          And so she brought me to Egypt, here. MENELAOS And so,
          as you also told me, she supplied
          a phantom image to take your place.

HELEN But in your house there is more, oh, more grief still.
       My mother . . . MENELAOS Yes? HELEN Is dead.

46

Believing in my disgrace,
with her own hands she tied the noose's knot.

MENELAOS Poor woman. And what of Hermione, our child?   740

HELEN The imagined dishonor of my marriage-bed
has left her stricken—childless and unwed.

MENELAOS O Paris, you have ruined and defiled
my house from roof to base;
yet you yourself were killed
and the bronze-armed Greeks in thousands had to die.

HELEN Accursed and star-crossed,
I was robbed by Hera of my country, bereft
of city and friends; above all, I lost
you on the day when I left   750
your home and bed—and all for a lie,
for it was only my name, only my name
that earned me an adulteress's shame.

CHORUS If only from now on you meet with luck,
that will be compensation for the past.

SERVANT Menelaos, let me deeper into your joy,
which I glimpse but don't yet fully understand.

MENELAOS By all means, old one, share the news with us.

SERVANT But isn't this the lady who presided
over the agony of the men at Troy?   760

MENELAOS No. We were tricked by the gods. The Helen we seized
was only a mischievous phantom made of air.

SERVANT What! All that pain endured for a mere ghost?

MENELAOS That was the work of Hera and her rivals.

47

SERVANT And so this lady here is your real wife?

MENELAOS She is. I say so; take my word for it.

SERVANT Daughter, the ways of God are intricate
and hard to fathom. With a curious wisdom
he disarranges everything to make
new patterns. Some attempt and strive and fail,   770
others effortlessly prosper, then one day
run into ruin, for no man is certain
of holding fortune steady in his hands.
You and your husband have had more than your share
of suffering—you had to stand against
a storm of words, and he a storm of spears.
When he fought hard he won nothing, and yet now
happiness of its own accord is his.
And so you never shamed your aged father
and your divine twin brothers, nor did you do   780
what the world said you did. In my mind's eye
I can see the day of your marriage, I remember
waving a torch and running beside the wheels
of the four yoked horses when you were a bride
being charioted by your husband Menelaos
from your grand house. You know, it's a bad servant
who doesn't take his master's life to heart,
share in his grief and celebrate his joy.
Though I was born a slave, with a slave's name,
my mind is my own and I should like to be ranked   790
among the noble slaves. Far better that way
than for one man to be twice handicapped—
having to obey the people round about him
and to be cursed with a servile spirit too.

MENELAOS Old fellow-soldier who with shield and spear
have done your stint of hardship in my service
and are now due for a ration of my luck,
go and report to the friends I left behind
our situation as you see it, the ticklish
corner we're in; tell them to go to the shore   800

and wait in readiness for the trial of strength
I can see coming, and to keep alert
to find some means of rescuing my wife
and escaping the barbarians, if we can,
to unite our strength and fortunes once again.

SERVANT   It shall be done, my lord. I do now see
how full of lies, how rotten the whole business
of prophecy is. There never was any sense
in watching sacrificial flames and listening
to the cries of birds—in fact the very notion   810
that birds help men is plain ridiculous.
Kalchas, our seer, looked on while his friends
died for a phantom, yet he gave the army
not a word, not a sign; and the same goes for Helenos
whose city it was we stormed and seized for nothing.
You may reply, "God willed it otherwise."
Then why do we mix with oracles? Much better
to sacrifice and pray to the gods and leave
prophets alone. Prophecy was invented
as a bait for gullible man, but no one ever   820
got rich without hard work by studying magic.
The best prophets are care and common sense.

LEADER   I heartily go along with the old man there.
Whoever makes the gods his friends has more
than a mere oracle inside his house.

                    Exit SERVANT right to pass the news along to his
                                                    shipmates.

HELEN   Well, then, so far so good. But now, my poor husband,
tell me how you've survived since Troy. I may not
profit by learning, but when your heart's involved
you long to share the troubles of those you love.

MENELAOS   One single question, yet it begs a hundred.   830
Must I describe our shipwrecks in the Aegean,
the false fires Nauplios kindled in Euboia,

the ports of Crete and Libya we put into,
and Perseus' lookout rock? Were I to give you
your fill of words I'd suffer in the telling
the same pains I suffered once in earnest
and double my sorrows by recalling them.

HELEN Your answer's better than my question was.
Leave all the rest, tell me just this: how long
did you wander driven over the sea's back?   840

MENELAOS We spent ten years at Troy; add on to those
seven summers and seven winters voyaging.

HELEN A long, grim time for you! And you've escaped
and reached here only to be faced with death!

MENELAOS Death? What do you mean? You chill my blood.

HELEN The master of this palace means to kill you.

MENELAOS What have I done to deserve to lose my life?

HELEN Your surprise arrival puts a stop to our wedding.

MENELAOS What? Someone here trying to marry my wife?

HELEN Yes, and to take me by force. I had to bear it.   850

MENELAOS What force? His own—or has he royal power?

HELEN He is the ruler here, the son of Proteus.

MENELAOS So that was what the old woman at the door meant!

HELEN What doors have you been knocking at in Egypt?

MENELAOS *points at the doors of the palace.*

MENELAOS These doors. And I was chased off like some beggar.

HELEN Not asking for charity? Oh, I feel the shame!

MENELAOS It amounted to that, though the word wasn't used.

HELEN Evidently you know the whole story.

MENELAOS I do. What I don't know is how far you've foiled them.

HELEN Then learn: my body's been kept chaste for you. 860

MENELAOS But how can I be sure? Sweet news if true!

HELEN You see this tomb, the seat of my despair?

MENELAOS Yes, and a couch of straw too. What's it for?

HELEN I sit there praying to escape this marriage.

MENELAOS Have you no altar? Or is this their custom?

HELEN I've been as safe as in our own gods' temples.

MENELAOS Then can't I bring you aboard and sail for home?

HELEN You'd be nearer to your grave than to my bed.

MENELAOS And so the most unhappy man alive.

HELEN Escape and save yourself. Don't be ashamed. 870

MENELAOS And leave you—when I sacked Troy for your sake?

HELEN Better than that my love should cause your death.

MENELAOS Cowardly advice to a veteran of Troy!

HELEN I suppose you want to kill the king. You couldn't.

MENELAOS And why not? Is his body weapon-proof?

HELEN You'll see. To attempt the impossible is folly.

MENELAOS So I meekly hold both hands out to be bound?

HELEN You're cornered. We must think up some way out.

MENELAOS I'd rather be killed in action than die tamely.

HELEN There's just one hope for us, a single chance.   880

MENELAOS Persuasion? Bribery? Or a stroke of daring?

HELEN If the king never learns of your arrival—

MENELAOS Who's going to tell him—even know my name?

HELEN He has an ally inside, with the power of a god.

MENELAOS You mean some private oracle in the palace?

HELEN I mean his sister, whom they call Theonöe.

MENELAOS An oracular-sounding name—but what does she do?

HELEN She knows all things. She'll tell her brother you're here.

MENELAOS And I shall be killed. I have no way of hiding.

HELEN But if we both appealed to her as suppliants—   890

MENELAOS To do what? What hope are you leading up to?

HELEN Not to inform her brother of your presence.

MENELAOS If we won her over, could we get away?

HELEN With her help, easily; in secret, no.

MENELAOS That's your task: woman to woman's the best way.

HELEN   I'll get to her and clasp her knees, I promise.

MENELAOS   But wait, what if she's deaf to our appeals?

HELEN   You die, and I am miserably forced to marry.

MENELAOS   Betrayer! The word "forced" is mere excuse.

HELEN   No! For I've solemnly sworn by your own head—   900

MENELAOS   Sworn what? To die? Never to swerve in love?

HELEN   To die by the same sword as you, and lie by you.

MENELAOS   To seal that pledge hold my right hand in yours.

HELEN   I do, and swear, if you die I die also.

MENELAOS   And I, if I lose you, shall take my life.

HELEN   How can we make an honorable ending?

MENELAOS   Here on this tomb. I'll kill you, then myself.
   But first I'll put up an almighty struggle
   for you and our marriage. Let who dares come near!
   I won't dishonor the name I won at Troy   910
   nor go back home to Greece with a great blot
   on my reputation. I was responsible
   for Thetis losing Achilles, I saw Ajax
   bleed on his own sword, I was there when Nestor
   was left without a son—am I the man, then,
   to count my wife not worth the price of death?
   Not I. If there are gods above and wise ones,
   they let the earth lie lightly on the brave man
   slain by his enemies, but the corpse of a coward
   they cast unburied on some barren reef.   920

LEADER   Dear Heaven, may the house of Tantalos
   be happy at last and freed of all its sorrows.

The doors of the palace begin to open, in preparation
for the arrival of the priestess and princess THEONÖE.

HELEN   O endless misery! Bad luck dogs me still.
Menelaos, we are trapped. Theonöe
the prophetess is coming out of the house—
I hear the sound of the doors being unbarred.
Fly! But what good will that do? Whether she's here
or somewhere else she can divine your presence.
I'm in despair—I am ruined. You escaped
from Troy, from one barbarian country, only   930
to meet with other, equally savage swords.

Enter THEONÖE, *center, solemnly, in the robes of a*
priestess. She is preceded by two handmaids, one of
whom carries a stemmed bowl in which a flame is visible,
and the other a torch. THEONÖE *addresses them in turn*
at 932 and 935 before turning to HELEN *at 940.*

THEONÖE   Lead on. Hold the bright torches up. Bring sulphur
to purify the air by holy ritual
that I may draw the untainted breath of heaven;
and if anyone with unhallowed foot has fouled
my path, be sure to purge the floor with fire,
grinding the pine-torch in, so I may pass.
Your holy chores completed, then take back
the flame to the palace hearth from where it came.
          Helen, what do you think of my prophecies now?   940
Without his ships, without his phantom wife,
Menelaos manifestly stands before you.
Unhappy man, to escape so many dangers
only to end up here without even knowing
which it's to be—sweet home or bitter Egypt.
This day the assembly of the gods will argue
your case in the court of Zeus. Your old foe, Hera,
is now your friend and wants to bring about
a safe return for you, and Helen with you,
that Greece may learn how Aphrodite's gift   950

to Paris was no gift, his bride no bride.
But Aphrodite wants to foil your journey
that the world may never know that when she purchased
the beauty-prize she paid for it in false coin.
It lies in my power either to destroy you,
as Aphrodite hopes, by telling my brother
of your arrival, or to side with Hera
and save your life by keeping it dark from him—
although my strict instructions were to report
if you touched Egypt on your voyage home.   960

THEONÖE *turns to the* CHORUS, *but the request she makes
is ignored and soon lapses.*

Will someone go and make known to my brother
Menelaos' presence, and so assure my safety?

HELEN *adopts an attitude of supplication toward* THE-
ONÖE, *which she maintains up to line 1016.*

HELEN Maiden, I fall to the ground in supplication
and clasp your knees, and in this humble posture,
for my sake and this man's—whom at long last
having won back I'm in immediate danger
of losing again, to death—ask you to spare us.
Now that my husband's found my loving arms,
save him, I beg you, don't inform your brother.
Don't sacrifice your piety to buy   970
a bad man's gratitude with a shameful deed.
God abominates violence; his commandment
to all of us is: get and enjoy possessions,
but not by robbery. For just as the sky
belongs to all men, so too does this earth
where each may fill his house with goods, so long as
they are his own and not snatched from his neighbor.
Although I've suffered in Egypt, in the end
it's proved a blessed chance that Hermes gave me
to your father to be kept safe for my husband,   980

who stands here eager to reclaim his own.
How can he if he's dead? And how could Proteus
pay what he owes, a live woman, to a corpse?
Consider the contract between man and god:
wouldn't both Hermes and the dead king wish
what's rightfully one man's to be given back?
I know they would. You mustn't give more weight
to a wild brother than an upright father.
You are a seer, you believe in the gods—
how can you break your father's just commitment
to keep the bad law of a lawless brother?   990
Shame!—to be privy to the thoughts of Fate
present and future, and not know what's wrong!
You see me dogged by misery, ringed by dangers—
save us, bestow this extra grace of fortune.
For the whole world hates Helen. All Greece knows me
as the wife who deceived her husband and eloped
to live in the golden mansions of the East.
But if I get back to Greece and Sparta again,
if they hear and see the truth—that they were ruined
by the trick of a god, that I never betrayed my loves—   1000
they'll restore me my good name: I'll see my daughter,
whom no man wants now, married and enjoy
the comfort and the wealth of my own house
far from this hateful beggary in exile.
If Menelaos had been killed abroad,
I should have rendered my service to the dead
with loving tears, in his absence. But he's here
and he's alive. Must he be taken from me?
No, prophetess. As a suppliant I implore you,
grant me this favor and in so doing follow   1010
your noble father's footsteps; for the child
of a fine man can win no glory greater
than matching the example of his life.

LEADER The words you have spoken, and you yourself still more,
arouse my pity. But how will Menelaos
argue to save his life? I long to hear.

MENELAOS *remains standing.*

MENELAOS I cannot bring myself to fall to the ground
and hug your knees and let loose floods of tears—
such abject, weak behavior would disgrace
the memory of Troy. And yet they say   1020
that high-born men in deep distress have wept
without dishonor. All the same, I spurn
this doubtful style of manhood. I choose courage.
If it seems right to you to save a stranger—
what's more, a man attempting to reclaim
his rightful wife—then give her back to me
and help us to escape. If not, it won't be
the first grief I've endured, or the last either;
but you will be seen to be an evil woman.
What I consider my rights and my deserts   1030
I'll tell you now, adding what seems most likely
to touch your heart—here, by your father's tomb.

MENELAOS *turns toward the tomb of Proteus.*

O ancient spirit, inmate of this marble,
I claim my debt from you—restore my wife
whom Zeus sent here to rest in your safe-keeping.
I know that, being dead, you'll lack the power
to hand her over yourself, but surely your daughter
will never deign to let her once great father
be summoned from his grave to hear his name
execrated? Now we are in her hands.   1040
     Hades, lord of the underworld, you too
I call upon for help. You have received
hundreds of men who fell before my sword,
all for this woman's sake: you have had your payment.
Now give me back those warriors alive
or else compel Theonöe to surpass
her father's piety by giving me Helen.

He turns away from the tomb and addresses THEONÖE.

If you and your brother steal my wife from me,
I'll tell you, as she failed to, what will happen.
Prophetess, you should know we're bound by oath: 1050
I've vowed to fight your brother to the death,
it's him or me—that's all there is to it.

                    MENELAOS *wields his sword demonstratively.*

If he won't meet me man to man and tries
to trap and starve us in our sanctuary,
I've sworn first to kill Helen and then thrust
this two-edged sword into my heart on the grave-slab
of Proteus here, till the gushing blood drips down;
and so we'll lie, two corpses, side by side
on the marble monument, to torment your conscience
forever and pollute your father's name.   1060
Neither your brother nor any man alive
is going to marry her—I shall take her with me,
home, if I can, and if not, to the dead.
But why am I saying all this? I should have won
more pity by recourse to woman's tears
than by this forceful speech. If you wish to, kill me—
but you will not kill your shame. Far better choice
to be persuaded by my arguments:
then you'll act justly and I'll have my wife.

LEADER Maiden, it rests with you to judge the case: 1070
        judge it so that all of us here feel pleased.

THEONÖE By nature and vocation I love piety;
         I cherish myself, and I would never sully
         my father's name or do my brother a favor
         at the cost of my own dishonor. In my heart
         there's a great shrine of Justice: I inherit it
         from my grandfather Nereus, and, Menelaos,
         I mean to keep it holy all my life.
         Since Hera wants to aid you, I shall cast
         my vote with Hera's. As for Aphrodite   1080

(may Love not be offended!), she has never
been a friend of mine, for I propose to stay
a virgin to the end. The reproach you aimed
at my father by this tomb hits me as well:
not to repay would be wrong. Were he alive,
I know he would restore you to each other.
For all the world, the dead as well as the living,
agrees that good and evil are rewarded.
The dead may not have living minds like ours,
but having once mixed with immortal ether   1090
they have immortal consciousness. Therefore,
not to prolong my speech, I shall keep silence
on the subject of your plea, I shall not become
an accomplice to my brother's wicked folly.
Indeed, however it may seem to the world,
in trying to steer him from impiety
to godliness I'm doing him a service.
As for escape, you must find some way yourselves:
I'll stand aside, aloof, and hold my tongue.
Begin with the gods. First pray to Aphrodite   1100
to allow you a safe journey home, and then
ask Hera to stay constant to you both
in her goodwill, on which deliverance hangs.
   O my dead father, while there's strength in me
your sacred memory shall not be profaned!

> Exit THEONÖE, center, with her retinue into the
> palace.

LEADER   The wicked never prosper in their ways:
   our hope of safety lies in doing right.

HELEN   We're safe as far as she's concerned, Menelaos.
   As for the rest, you must come up with a plan
   by which we can effect our joint escape.   1110

MENELAOS   Then listen to me. You've been here a long time—
   you've grown familiar with the palace servants?

HELEN   Why do you ask? You seem to raise the hope
of doing something positive to help us.

MENELAOS   Could you persuade one of the grooms in charge
of the four-horse chariots to give us one?

HELEN   I could; but how can we escape by land
over the huge, unknown Egyptian plains?

MENELAOS   You're right, we can't. Well, then, I'll hide in the palace
and kill the king with this sword. What do you say?   1120

HELEN   Theonöe wouldn't sanction that; she'd break
her silence rather than let you kill her brother.

MENELAOS   What's more, we haven't even got a ship
for our flight. The sea has claimed the one we had.

HELEN   Listen—a woman can plan wisely too.
Will you let me, as a ruse, report you dead?

MENELAOS   Ominous word! But if I'll be the gainer
I'm willing to be called dead when I'm not.

HELEN   Good; then I'll act the woman's part, with dirges
and a shaved head, for the irreligious king.   1130

MENELAOS   But how will this trick help our combined escape?
It's rather an old-fashioned one, you know.

HELEN   I'll tell him you were drowned at sea and ask him
for permission to erect a monument.

MENELAOS   Suppose he agrees, how can we save ourselves
with an empty tomb when we haven't got a ship?

HELEN   I'll insist on a ship, so that your robes and jewels
can duly be consigned to the sea's hands.

MENELAOS Perfect—except for one thing: if he orders
a ceremony on land, your pretext fails.   1140

HELEN But I'll make out that it isn't the Greek custom
to bury ashore those who were lost at sea.

MENELAOS Another good idea. And I shall join you
on board the ship to help you with the ritual.

HELEN Of course you must, you above all, and with you
those of your sailors who survived the wreck.

MENELAOS Once I've a ship at anchor, I'll have my men
embark, armed with their swords, in fighting order.

HELEN You must arrange all that. I'll simply pray
for favorable winds. Let the ship run!   1150

MENELAOS It shall. The gods are about to end my troubles.
But who will you say told you that I was dead?

HELEN You! I'll pretend you were the sole survivor
of Menelaos' crew, and saw him drown.

MENELAOS Yes, and these rags of sail I've got wrapped round me
will lend color to your story of the wreck.

HELEN They're handy now, though your clothes were a sad
loss then.
That ill wind could still blow us some good.

MENELAOS Shall I go indoors with you, or would it be better
to sit here quietly beside the tomb?   1160

HELEN Stay here. If he resorts to viciousness
the tomb, as well as your own sword, will protect you.
Meanwhile I'll enter the palace, cut my hair off,
change this white robe for mourning black, then scratch

my cheeks with my nails till the skin shows blood.
For now everything hangs in the balance; the scales
must tilt one way or the other, as I see it:
either I die, caught out in my deception,
or else we reach home, and I have saved your life.
        O Hera, queen of heaven, you who lie   1170
in the bed of Zeus, we two pitiful creatures
lift up our hands to your star-embroidered halls
and beg for a calm after our storm of troubles.
And you, Dione's child, great Aphrodite,
who gained the prize of beauty for the price
of my false marriage, please do not destroy me.
You loaded me with enough shame before,
when you lent my name, not me, to an alien people.
If you desire to kill me, let me die
in my own land. You deal in passions, lies,   1180
crooked intrigues, love-charms, and drugs that lead
to murder in families—why are you never sated
with working mischief? If you could only be
reasonable, there'd be no other god
so sweet to mortals. I acknowledge it.

Exit HELEN, *center, into the palace; the* CHORUS *this time
                        remains, as does* MENELAOS.

CHORUS   Perched among leafy tresses
            of olive or of oak,
         from deep in your melodious recesses,
         sweetest and saddest of birds, you I invoke.
         Come, nightingale, summon a note   1190
         from your brown, rippling throat
         to match my voice as I sing
         of unhappy Helen's tears
       . and the lamentable suffering
       . of the men of Troy who faced the Grecian spears
         when Paris, fatally wed
         but favorably sped
         by Aphrodite, drove his intruding oar

over the plains of foam,
taking you, Helen, far, far from home   1200
to prove a murderous bride
for all the sons of Priam who have died
in war, in war.

Spears were thrust, rocks were hurled,
and thousands of Greeks now haunt the underworld,
whose desolate wives have shorn
their hair, whose widowed homes still mourn.
And Nauplios, single-handed in his skiff,
when he lit up with his bright beacon-fire
sea-girt Euboia—star that proved a liar—   1210
wrecked many more,
doom-dashed on every rock and cliff
around Kaphereos on the Aegean shore.
And harborless and unkind
to Menelaos were the bluffs of Malea when the wind
of winter drove him from Sparta with, on board,
the prize of his foreign raid
(oh, unrewarding reward—
war with the Greeks!), the mocking shade,
the phantom Helen that Hera made.   1220

What is god, what is not god, what lies in between
man and god? Who on this earth, after searching,
can claim to have been
to the end of that question's tortuous lane?
For every man has seen
the plans of the gods lurching
here and there and back again
in unexpected and absurd
vicissitudes. O Helen, you were conceived
in Leda's womb by Zeus winged like a bird,   1230
yet from the rooftops of Greece you have been
        proclaimed
a wicked woman who deceived
her husband, shamed

honor, and erred
against the laws of God and man.
Discover who can
certainty in the utterance of mankind.
For myself, I find
truth only in God's word.

Madmen, all who seek glory in war,   1240
trusting in ignorance
to the sheer weight of the lance
to end mortal debate!
If battle and blood are to settle the score,
grief and hate
will never leave the cities of men. Through strife
such men have found
cramped sleeping room, a Trojan burial mound,
who might by words have learnt
some way to compound   1250
the quarrel over Menelaos' wife—
you, Helen! Now they lie in the domain
of the god of death, and pouncing fire has burnt,
as if Zeus had hurled his bolt, those walls to the ground,
while you endure a pitiable life
of pain, of pain.

Enter THEOKLYMENOS, *left. He is accompanied by at-*
tendants who are carrying hunting gear; there are hounds
on the leash. The retinue is speedily dispatched into the
palace (at 1261-62). THEOKLYMENOS *first stops at the*
tomb of his father, and soon notices (1271-72) that
*   HELEN is not to be found.*

THEOKLYMENOS Hail, monument of my father, which I sited
at my main gateway for this very purpose—
that, entering or leaving, I, your son,
Theoklymenos might thus salute you, Proteus.   1260
        You servants, take the dogs and hunting-nets
inside the palace, to their proper places.

I've often criticized myself: I've failed,
feebly, to punish criminals with death.
And now I discover some Greek has landed here
in broad daylight and given my scouts the slip—
a spy no doubt, or somebody trying by stealth
to kidnap Helen. He's a corpse as soon as he's found!
Hah!
It seems I've arrived too late. The plot's accomplished.   1270
There's no one here—the daughter of Tyndareus
has left the tomb and been smuggled out of the country!

THEOKLYMENOS *bangs on the doors of the palace; ser-
             vants appear, and disappear, to do his bidding.*

Ho, there, unbar the doors, open the stables,
bring out the chariots! My hoped-for bride
shall not escape for lack of hard pursuit.

                              Re-enter HELEN, *center.*

But hold! The woman I was looking for
hasn't got away. She's here, in the palace doorway.
        Helen, you've changed from white clothes into
              black!
And why have you put iron scissors to your head
and cut short your proud hair? Your cheeks are running   1280
with fresh tears—why are you weeping? Has a dream
overshadowed your mind and made you sad?
Or have you had heartbreaking news from home?

HELEN My lord and master—as I must call you now—
      I'm lost. My hopes are dead, and so am I.

THEOKLYMENOS What sort of trouble are you in? What's happened?

HELEN My Menelaos—oh, how can I say the words?—is dead.

THEOKLYMENOS Though the news gives me hope, I cannot rejoice.
             How do you know this? Did Theonöe tell you?

HELEN Yes—and a witness too, who saw him die.   1290

THEOKLYMENOS Somebody who can vouch for it—is he here?

HELEN He's here; but how I wish him somewhere else!

THEOKLYMENOS Who is he? Where is he now? I want the facts.

HELEN There he is—there, cowering beside the tomb.

> HELEN *points to* MENELAOS *who, once again, is partially concealed near the tomb and is cringing there pitiably.*

THEOKLYMENOS By Apollo, what a sight! The man's in rags.

HELEN Alas, my husband must have looked as wretched.

THEOKLYMENOS Who *is* this man? Where did he come here from?

HELEN He's a Greek, from aboard the same ship as my husband.

THEOKLYMENOS How does he say that Menelaos died?

HELEN The saddest death—drowned in the deep, salt sea.   1300

THEOKLYMENOS In what wild waters was he voyaging?

HELEN He was wrecked on the harborless cliffs of Libya.

THEOKLYMENOS How comes it that his shipmate here survived?

HELEN Sometimes the low- are luckier than the high-born.

THEOKLYMENOS Where did he leave the wrecked ship before landing?

HELEN Where I hope it may rot. (*Half aside*) Forgive me,
         Menelaos.

THEOKLYMENOS Menelaos is dead. What boat did this fellow come in?

HELEN Some sailors found him and picked him up, he says.

THEOKLYMENOS And the evil phantom sent in your place to Troy . . . ?

HELEN The image of air? It has vanished back to air.   1310

THEOKLYMENOS O Troy and Priam, all destroyed for nothing!

HELEN I, too, shared disaster with the Trojans.

THEOKLYMENOS Did he leave your husband's body unburied, or—

HELEN Unburied, unburied. And I weep for that.

THEOKLYMENOS So this is why you've cut your yellow curls?

HELEN I loved him and still do, wherever he is.

THEOKLYMENOS Should I believe you? Are these tears sincere?

HELEN Would it be easy to deceive your sister?

THEOKLYMENOS It wouldn't. . . . Well, is this tomb to be your home?

HELEN In avoiding you I keep faith with my husband.   1320

THEOKLYMENOS Why taunt and tease me? Let the dead man be.

HELEN I shall. I do. Prepare now for our wedding.

THEOKLYMENOS Consent was long in coming, but I'm glad.

HELEN Do you know what we ought to do? Forget the past.

THEOKLYMENOS On what terms? For one gift deserves another.

HELEN Let us conclude a truce. Give me your friendship.

THEOKLYMENOS I hereby consign our quarrel to the winds.

HELEN Since you're my friend, I fall at your feet and beg—

HELEN *falls to her knees.*

THEOKLYMENOS What do you beg, as a suppliant on your knees?

HELEN I wish to . . . may I bury my dead husband?   1330

THEOKLYMENOS What, a grave without a corpse? Bury a shadow?

HELEN In Greece, when a man is lost at sea, the custom—

THEOKLYMENOS Yes? Pelops' people are expert in these matters.

HELEN Is to perform the rites with an empty shroud.

THEOKLYMENOS Give him a tomb by all means. Choose a site.

HELEN That's not our way of burying the drowned.

THEOKLYMENOS What *is*, then? I'm quite ignorant of your customs.

HELEN We take the gifts we owe them out to sea.

THEOKLYMENOS How can I help? What do you need for the dead?

MENELAOS *stands up and prepares to take part in the
dialogue.*

HELEN This man knows, I don't—I've been lucky till now.   1340

THEOKLYMENOS Well, stranger, you have brought me news that's
welcome.

MENELAOS Not welcome to me—nor to the dead man either.

THEOKLYMENOS But tell me: how do you bury those that are drowned?

MENELAOS It all depends how rich or poor they are.

THEOKLYMENOS For Helen's sake no expense shall be spared.

MENELAOS First we offer the powers below some blood.

THEOKLYMENOS Which animal's? Tell me and I shall oblige.

MENELAOS You choose. Whatever you provide will do.

THEOKLYMENOS In Egypt a horse or bull is customary.

MENELAOS Make sure, though, that the beast you offer is flawless.   1350

THEOKLYMENOS We have plenty of those among our splendid herds.

MENELAOS We need a bier, too, for the absent body.

THEOKLYMENOS You shall be given it. What else should one supply?

MENELAOS Bronze arms and armor: he was war's companion.

THEOKLYMENOS Panoply fit for a Greek king—I'll provide them.

MENELAOS And fruit and flowers, whatever your soil produces.

THEOKLYMENOS And then? How do you give all this to the sea?

MENELAOS There has to be a boat, and rowers too.

THEOKLYMENOS And how far from the land does it have to go?

MENELAOS Till the foam of the oars is hardly visible.   1360

THEOKLYMENOS Why? What's the purpose of this strange Greek ritual?

MENELAOS To avoid foul blood being washed back to the shore.

THEOKLYMENOS A fast Phoenician vessel's at your disposal.

MENELAOS That's kind of you—and kind to Menelaos.

THEOKLYMENOS But can't you manage this? Do you need her help?

MENELAOS His mother, wife, or child must see it done.

THEOKLYMENOS You mean, this burial is her painful duty?

MENELAOS To cheat the dead of their due offends the gods.

THEOKLYMENOS She may go, then. I would wish my wife to be pious.
Enter the palace, select your gifts for the dead;   1370
I shall not send you from Egypt empty-handed
if you help Helen. You have brought me heartening
        news:
in place of these rags—for I note your sorry state—
you shall have food and clothes for your passage home.
And you, unhappy Helen, don't weary yourself
with useless tears. Menelaos has met his doom.
Crying won't bring your husband back to life.

MENELAOS You know your task now, lady. You must show love
to the husband you have and let the other go.
Things being as they are, it's your best course.   1380
If I manage to get safely back to Greece,
I'll kill the old slanders about you. Only be
the true wife to your husband that you should be.

HELEN I shall; and you will be close enough to see
that my lord will have no reason for complaint.
But now, poor man, go indoors, take a bath
and change your clothes. You won't have long to wait
for your reward—for you'll be that much keener
to serve my dearest Menelaos, knowing
that I am ready to give you what I owe you.   1390

Exeunt HELEN, MENELAOS, and THEOKLYMENOS, center,
all into the palace. There is a pause in the action while
                the CHORUS sings a long ode.

CHORUS Long ago
        the Mountain Mother of the gods ran to and fro
        on frantic feet, combing the forest glades,
        the brooks and rivers and cascades,
        even the waves of the thunder-throated sea,
        anguish-wild,
        to find her stolen child
        whose unutterable name is mystery.
        Shrilly clamored the bronze, sonorous
        cymbals when the goddess yoked her lion-drawn car   1400
        in search of Persephone, the maid
        ravished from the circles of the dancing-chorus;
        and whirlwind-footed to her aid
        rushed Artemis with her arrows of war,
        Athene with her spear and Gorgon's eyes.
        But watching from his throne in the skies,
        Zeus ordained things otherwise.

        When the Great Mother ceased her hard,
        sore-footed, world-wandering quest
        for her daughter and her daughter's cunning thief,   1410
        she climbed Mount Ida, she crossed
        the snow-blooming crest
        where the upland nymphs keep guard,
        threw herself down among the winter-white,
        rock-strewn thickets, and in her grief
        unleashed a universal blight.
        She scorched the ungreen fields,
        starving men of the yields
        of each expected crop;
        to injure the flocks she dried   1420
        the juicy fodder of the curling leaf;
        through her, the child in the womb died,
        life in the cities came to a stop,
        gods were denied
        their rites, and altars their burnt offerings;
        at source she choked the springs
        of their jetting, shining water—

all in bitter, insufferable grief
for her lost daughter.

But then,   1430
when she had brought to a halt the feasts that men
share with the gods, Zeus, to assuage
her black, impassioned sense of wrong,
spoke out: "Demeter is savage with rage
for her lost child.
Go, sacred Graces, go, Muses, and with your art,
with the shock of music, with dance and with song
shift the mood of her heart."
The first of the immortals then to come
was the loveliest. Aphrodite seized   1440
the rumbling, bronze-voiced cymbal and the hide-
        stretched drum,
and the Mother smiled
and took the flute in her hands and, beguiled
by its deep, loud throb, was eased.

Helen, you did not do right,
you committed a sin:
in your chamber you lit an unholy flame
and, child, you failed to honor the name
of the Great Mother, and she avenged the slight.
For great is the power of the dappled skin   1450
of the fawn which her worshippers wear,
of the vivid green
of the ivy wreath on the sacred wand they bear,
of the frenzied tambourine
whirled and brandished high in the air,
of the wild tossed hair
which her reveling devotees shake,
of their nights spent rapt and awake . . .
Your beauty, Helen, was all you gloried in.

                                        Re-enter HELEN, center.

HELEN   Friends, things have gone well for us in the palace.   1460
        The daughter of Proteus, questioned by her brother,
        acted her part in our plot and said not a word
        about my husband's presence; indeed, to help me,
        she said he was dead, out of the sunlight, buried.
        Meanwhile my lord has made a lucky haul:
        the arms that he was supposed to sink in the sea
        he's wearing himself, his strong left arm in the
              shield-band,
        his right hand with a spear, to all appearance
        as if he were about to play his role
        in the burial ceremony.   1470

        Re-enter MENELAOS, center. He has shed his rags and
        now stands in the panoply of the warrior he is about
                                      once again to become.

                    So here he comes,
        conveniently armed, spoiling for battle
        like a man who means to hang victorious trophies
        over the corpses of a thousand Egyptians
        the moment we get aboard and use our oars.
        I myself, in place of those rags from the wreck,
        have given him new clothes as well as the bath
        his body had long craved, in sweet, fresh water.
        But look! Here is the prince who thinks he holds
        my instant marriage in the palm of his hand.
        I must be silent. I beg you, be my friends   1480
        and guard your tongues; and then, if we escape,
        one day we may contrive to save you too.

        Re-enter THEOKLYMENOS, center, again attended by a
        retinue of slaves bearing gifts for the "funeral," who
        however mostly immediately leave the stage to the right.

THEOKLYMENOS   To your work, men. Do as the stranger tells you
        and take the funeral offerings to the shore.
        Helen—don't take these words amiss—stay here,
        be ruled by me. Whether or not you're present

at the rite, you honor your husband just the same.
My fear is that, driven mad by memories
of love, in a fit of passionate devotion
you'll throw yourself in the sea; for the grief you show   1490
for a man who's dead elsewhere is too intense.

HELEN My new-found husband, I am duty-bound
to revere the memory, the intimacy
of my first marriage. I've loved Menelaos
so much that I could die with him—but then
what benefit would my death bring him in death?
No, let me go in person and offer the gifts
due to the departed. May the gods reward you—
and this stranger too, since he's been helping us—
with all I could wish for you both. And for your   1500
     kindness
to me and to Menelaos you shall find me
exactly the sort of wife that you deserve;
for all that's happening points to a good end.
Now, please give someone orders to put a ship
at our disposal for the funeral rite,
and then my gratitude will be complete.

THEOKLYMENOS *turns to an attendant.*

THEOKLYMENOS You there, go and get ready a fifty-oared
Sidonian galley with a crew of rowers!

HELEN *points to* MENELAOS.

HELEN This stranger will be in charge of the sea-burial—
won't he have command of the ship as well?   1510

THEOKLYMENOS He will indeed; my sailors must obey him.

HELEN Repeat that, so that it's clearly understood.

THEOKLYMENOS They must obey him. Shall I say it a third time?

HELEN   Blessings upon your hopes—and my hopes too!

THEOKLYMENOS   Don't spoil your beauty now with too much crying.

HELEN   Today will show how grateful to you I am.

THEOKLYMENOS   The dead are nothing; tears are wasted effort.

HELEN   I'm thinking of this world as well as the other.

THEOKLYMENOS   You will find me as good a man as Menelaos.

HELEN   You *have* been good. Now all I need is luck.   1520

THEOKLYMENOS   That lies with you. Be friends with me, you'll have it.

HELEN   I don't need to be taught how to love my friends.

THEOKLYMENOS   Shall I help you by accompanying you myself?

HELEN   No, sire. A king should never serve his servants.

THEOKLYMENOS   Very well. I need not bother myself further
with your Greek ceremonies. My house is clean—
it wasn't here that Menelaos died.
Go, one of you, and tell all my chief subjects
to bring their wedding-gifts inside the palace.
Let the land ring with music and with songs   1530
in celebration, in congratulation
of the marriage between Helen and myself.
Meanwhile, stranger, put all this in the hands
of the sea, in honor of her former husband,
then hurry back again, bringing my wife,
and share in our wedding banquet; after which
either sail home or stay here at your pleasure.

Exit THEOKLYMENOS *center into the palace.*

75

MENELAOS O Zeus, known as our father, wisest of gods,
          look down on us, grant us respite from pain.
          As we drag our difficulties up the slope   1540
          reach us your hand—one touch of your fingertip
          and we're there, at the summit, where we hope to be.
          I've done my share of suffering in the past.
          You gods, I've called upon you many times
          in tones that may have pleased you or displeased you,
          and I don't deserve to spend my whole life staggering
          under catastrophe, I ought to be able
          to walk upright. Indulge my prayer this once
          and I shall live a happy man forever.

          Exeunt HELEN *and* MENELAOS *right, toward the waiting
                                                          ship.*

CHORUS Speed home, speed home,   1550
          galley of Sidon, mother of oars loved by the foam,
          dance-leader when the dolphins revel
          and the winds are fair and the waves lie level.
          May Galaneia, goddess of calms, the sea's
          grey-green daughter, speak words like these:
          "Spread the sails wide to the salt breeze,
          sailors, tug at the oars,
          tug at the oars till you have grounded
          the ship, with Helen, on kind Greek shores,
          in the city that Perseus founded."   1560

          There, Helen, you may meet
          your brothers' wives beside the swirling water
          of Eurotas; you may come in time to join the dance
          before Athene's temple, or to share the night of joy
          when Spartans celebrate the boy
          whom, challenged to compete,
          Apollo killed with the discus by mischance,
          and for whose sake the son of Zeus proclaimed
          throughout the land a day
          of revelry and sacrificial slaughter;   1570
          and the child you left when you went away,

for whom no bridal torch has ever flamed—
you may see her, Hermione, your daughter.

Oh, to have wings! Our prayer
is to be high in the air
over Libya with the flocks who escape the rains
of winter and in close ranks
follow the eldest, the captain bird,
whose clear whistle, always heard,
leads them over the deserts and the corn-green plains.   1580
O long-necked voyagers, O cranes,
who partner the clouds in their sky-races,
travel through the starry spaces,
under the Pleiads at their zenith, under Orion burning
in the middle of the night,
and when you reach the banks
of Eurotas, alight
and trumpet the tidings of joy—
that Menelaos has taken the city of Troy,
that Menelaos is returning.   1590

Come with the speed of your horses,
O sons of Tyndareus, sky-inhabiting pair,
rush through the air,
under the glittering, whirling courses
of the stars; champions of Helen, ride
over the grey-green swell of the tide,
over the dark-skinned
backs of the waves and the white jags of foam,
bringing the fresh and welcome wind
that comes from Zeus and takes the sailor home;   1600
banish the cloud of ill-fame
that has shadowed your sister ever since
men's tongues coupled her name
in scandal with a foreign prince;
dissolve the guilt
she has borne as punishment
for the quarrel on Ida, even though she never went
to Troy and never saw the towers Apollo built.

Enter THEOKLYMENOS *center from the palace, as a* MES-
SENGER *bursts in right, from the shore. Before* THEOKLY-
MENOS *can speak, the agitated* MESSENGER *bursts into
breathless speech.*

MESSENGER   My lord, the news I'm just about to tell you
             is utterly unexpected—and disastrous.   1610

THEOKLYMENOS What is it? MESSENGER You may as well start looking
             for a new bride. Helen has left the country.

THEOKLYMENOS Left! On wings, I suppose? Or did she walk?

MESSENGER   She was carried off in a ship by Menelaos—
             the man who brought the report of his own death.

THEOKLYMENOS This is appalling news. What sort of transport
             did they get away in? It's unbelievable!

MESSENGER   The transport you supplied him with. In short,
             he went off with *your* sailors in *your* ship.

THEOKLYMENOS How? I want to know how! For it surpasses   1620
             the bounds of my belief that a lone man
             could outwit a whole crew—and you were one of them!

MESSENGER   When the daughter of Zeus had left this royal house
             and was being escorted seawards, she adopted
             a graceful, mincing walk—it was clever acting—
             and set up a widow's wailing for the husband
             who, far from being dead, was right beside her.
             At last we reached your dockyard and hauled down
             a brand-new, fifty-oared Sidonian galley
             complete with benches. Each man did his job: 1630
             one fitted the mast in position, one arranged
             the oars, one furled the white sails, and the steersman
             lowered the rudders by the guiding-ropes.
             While all this work was going on, some Greeks,

sailors of Menelaos—they must have been
watching and biding their time—approached the shore:
fine-looking men, but dirty and disheveled,
wearing the rags of castaways. Seeing them,
the son of Atreus put on for our benefit
a show of commiseration. "Men," he called,   1640
"you have my sympathy. You look like Greeks.
What ship? How were you wrecked? Since you've
        arrived,
would you be willing to help in the burial
of Menelaos, lost at sea, whom Helen—
this lady here—is honoring with a tomb?"
Next thing, they'd shed some hypocritical tears
and come on board, carrying the sea-gifts
for Menelaos. Now we got suspicious
and muttered to one another about the crowd
of extra passengers, but all the same,   1650
remembering your orders, we kept quiet:
your guest was to be in absolute command,
you'd said—the whole disaster's due to that.
Anyway, the cargo being fairly light,
we easily hauled it aboard—but not the bull,
who pawed and slithered and balked at the straight
        gangplank,
bellowed and rolled his eyes and humped his back
and squinted down his horns and wouldn't allow
anyone to touch him. At which Helen's husband
shouted, "Takers of Troy, come on, why can't you   1660
lift up the bull the Greek way, on strong shoulders,
and carry him for'ard? He's our sacrifice."
And he drew his sword. They obeyed. They seized,
        hoisted,
and manhandled the bull onto the deck.
        At last, when the ship had taken on all cargo
and Helen with her dainty feet had mounted
every rung of the ladder, she sat down
on the quarter-deck, with her so-called "dead" husband.
The rest of the Greeks ranged themselves, two in a row,

on either side along the bulkheads, hiding   1670
swords under their clothes; and soon the waves
echoed as we took up the bosun's chant.
When we'd got out to sea—not too far out,
yet not too near the shore—our steersman asked,
"Shall we keep going, sir, or will this do?
You're in command here." Menelaos answered,
"This is far enough," and, taking his sword in hand,
worked his way to the prow, stood poised to strike,
then without mention of any dead man's name
cut the bull's throat, with a prayer: "Lord of the ocean,   1680
Poseidon, and you stainless Nereids,
convey me safely, and my wife with me,
away from Egypt to the shores of Nauplia."
A stream of blood jetted into the water—
a good omen for the Greek. Then one of us
spoke up and said, "There's treachery aboard!
Let's make for the shore. Row about to the right!
Put the helm over, someone!" The son of Atreus,
standing there after slaughtering the bull,
yelled to his men, "What are you waiting for,   1690
heroes of Greece? Kill these Egyptian dogs,
cut them to bits and throw them in the sea!"
In reply our captain roared out to your sailors,
"Come on! Find weapons, grab the end of a spar,
break up a seat, wrench an oar out of the rowlocks
and smash the heads of these accursed strangers!"
Every man sprang to his feet, we with nothing
but timber from the ship, they with their swords.
Soon the decks were awash with blood, while Helen
shouted encouragement from the stern: "Where now   1700
is the reputation that you won at Troy?
Show these barbarians!" It happened quickly:
some fell, some kept their feet, and you could see
dead men lying all round. Being fully armed,
Menelaos, wherever he saw his friends hard-pressed,
brought his sword-arm into play. In the end he swept
the benches clear of rowers, went to the rudder
and ordered the helmsman to steer straight for Greece.

They hoisted sail, and the wind blew in their favor.
    And so they've escaped from Egypt. I myself   1710
avoided death by climbing down the anchor
into the sea. I was half-dead when a fisherman
picked me up and brought me ashore; and so
I give you the news. Healthy mistrust, I've learnt,
is the quality that stands one in best stead.

LEADER I would never have dreamt, my lord, that Menelaos
could have been here unknown to you and me.

Exit MESSENGER, *right.*

THEOKLYMENOS Shame and misery, to be outwitted by a woman!
My bride has escaped. If pursuit could overhaul them,
I'd spare no effort, I'd soon seize those Greeks.   1720
As it is, I'll take revenge on my treacherous sister,
who saw Menelaos in the house and said nothing.
Never again will she cheat men with her prophecies!

THEOKLYMENOS *starts toward the palace, but the* CHORUS
stands in his way.

LEADER Where are you going, my lord? To commit a murder?

THEOKLYMENOS Where justice beckons me. Out of my way!

CHORUS A hasty, terrible crime! We clutch your robes.

THEOKLYMENOS Does a slave command his master? LEADER We are right.

THEOKLYMENOS But you do me wrong. Unless you let me—LEADER No!

THEOKLYMENOS Kill my vile sister—LEADER God-fearing, not vile.

THEOKLYMENOS Who betrayed me—LEADER Noble betrayal! A good   1730
        deed!

THEOKLYMENOS And gave my bride to a man—LEADER Who had first
        claim.

THEOKLYMENOS Over what's mine? LEADER Her father gave her to him.

THEOKLYMENOS Fortune gave her to me. LEADER And Fate removed her.

THEOKLYMENOS You're not my judge. LEADER I am, if I judge better.

THEOKLYMENOS So I'm overruled as king? LEADER Not when you're just.

THEOKLYMENOS You seem in love with dying. LEADER Kill me, then.
While we stand here you shall not kill your sister.
Kill me! The noblest thing a slave can do
is die with honor for the sake of his master.

The DIOSKOUROI, KASTOR and POLYDEUKES, appear in the
air above the palace, swung forward by the mēchanē, a
kind of crane fixed to the top of the stage buildings; in
this case, they may have been represented as riding on
horses. KASTOR alone speaks.

KASTOR Theoklymenos, King of Egypt, moderate   1740
your wrath: it is wrongly aimed. We who address you
are the Heavenly Twins, whom Leda once gave birth to
with Helen, who has now fled your house.
The lost marriage at which you rage was never
destined to be, nor did Theonöe,
the Nereid's daughter, wrong you when she honored
the command of both her father and the gods.
Until this day it had always been ordained
that she should live in your palace; but once Troy's
foundations were uprooted, she was meant   1750
to return home and share her husband's roof.
So sheathe that black sword pointed at your sister,
and own that what she did was wisely done.
We who were given the power of gods by Zeus
would have rescued her long ago had we not been
weaker than Destiny and the other gods,
who both alike willed that these things should be.
Those words were for you. Now I shall speak to
Helen.

Sail with your husband; you shall have fair winds;
we, your brothers, the Guardians, will escort you,   1760
skimming the waves on our horses. And one day,
when you complete the course of human life,
you shall be called divine along with us,
share our libations and be entertained,
like the Dioskouroi, with feasts and worship
from the race of men. For that is Zeus's will.
Where Hermes, when he snatched you up from Sparta,
marked the first stage of your skyborne flight and hid you
to foil your marriage to Paris—I mean the island
that sits like a sentinel opposite Attica—   1770
shall be known by the world as *Helen*, for its part
in sheltering your god-abducted beauty.
And the gods have granted wandering Menelaos
life after death in the Islands of the Blest.
Heaven never hates the high-born, but it's true,
they're given more trials than the nameless crowd.

THEOKLYMENOS O sons of Zeus and Leda, I abandon
my old quarrel with you over your sister.
If it's the will of the gods, let her go home.
Theonöe I spare. I recognize,   1780
and you should know, that you are both blood-brothers
of the best, most virtuous sister in the world.
Rejoice, therefore, in Helen's noble mind—
there are few women like her—and farewell.

CHORUS The divine will shows
itself in many forms. The gods dispose
many things unexpectedly, and what we base
certainty on may never take place.
God finds a way
for the event no man foreknows.   1790
So ends our play.

Exeunt omnes: THEOKLYMENOS *and the* CHORUS *retire
into the palace as the* DIOSKOUROI *are swung back and out
of sight by the* mēchanē.

NOTES AND GLOSSARY

NOTES

As noted in the Introduction, we have in general followed the text of G. Murray (Oxford, 1913), as used and sometimes altered or improved by A. M. Dale in her commentary (Oxford, 1967). In the case of significant divergences, brief comments will be found in these notes.

The notes do not, of course, constitute anything like a commentary. They mainly attempt to explain some points of difficulty or obscurity (textual or contextual); to draw attention to some matters of dramatic technique and stagecraft; and to show how Euripides constantly harps on the appearance/reality theme.

FAMILY TREES

1.

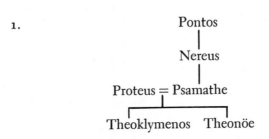

```
          Pontos
            |
          Nereus
            |
   Proteus = Psamathe
      ┌─────┴─────┐
Theoklymenos   Theonöe
```

2.

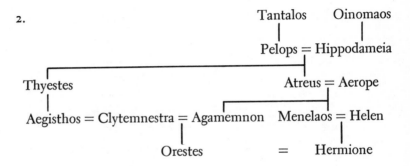

```
                              Tantalos   Oinomaos
                                 |           |
                              Pelops = Hippodameia
         ┌────────────────────────────┘
      Thyestes                        Atreus = Aerope
         |                           ┌────┴────┐
Aegisthos = Clytemnestra = Agamemnon  Menelaos = Helen
                    |                      |
                 Orestes        =       Hermione
```

3.

Thestios
|
Leda = Tyndareus or Zeus

Kastor   Pollux   Clytemnestra   Helen

4.

Zeus
|
Dardanos
|
Priam = Hecuba

Paris   Helenos

5.

Danaos
|
Akrisios
|
Danaë = Zeus
|
Perseus = Andromeda

6.

Poseidon
|
Neleus
|
Nestor
|
Antilochos

7.

Psamathe = Aiakos   Nereus
| |
Phokos   Telamon   Peleus = Thetis
|
Ajax   Teucer   Achilles

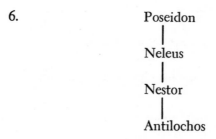
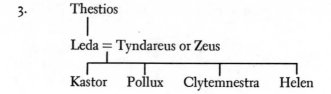
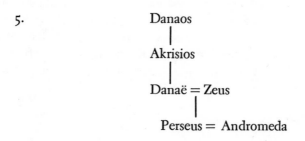
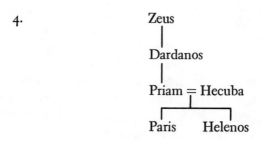

1-172 Prologue The situation, with Helen standing or sitting by the tomb of Proteus, is similar to that with which *Andromache* opens, where the heroine has taken refuge at a shrine of Thetis. Necessary as the prologue was at a time when, of course, there was no playbill or program (and this is especially true in a play such as *Helen*, where the author treats the myth in a decidedly unorthodox way, with a consequently greater need for explanation to the audience), Teucer is a somewhat unsatisfactory figure, dramatically speaking. He appears from nowhere, disappears into the same nowhere, and is not heard of again.

18 *There's an old story* Already the note of scepticism appears; the distinction between appearance and reality, so crucial and central to this play, is made over two dozen times in the course of it.

26 *Mount Ida* Of course, the Trojan Ida rather than the perhaps better-known Cretan one.

36ff. *not the real me . . . possesses only his belief* These are the bones of the story as told by Stesichorus; for a full and clear account, see Dale, Introduction, pp. xvii ff. The word for belief, *dokēsis*, is not a common one and may have something of a philosophical flavor.

41ff. *relieve the cumbered earth* The account of overpopulation as the cause of the Trojan War goes back a long way—in fact to the *Cypria*, ascribed to Stasinus. Euripides, ever the rationalist, seems to have favored it: he refers to it both in *Orestes* and *Electra*. The *mightiest Greek* (43) is Achilles.

94ff. *No wonder, then* The dialogue, in stichomythia, is confused and almost certainly corrupt between here and 96. It may be that a line has fallen out and been clumsily replaced; we have omitted one line which is almost certainly an interpolation (86 in Murray's text).

107 *one of Helen's suitors* Although this is inconsistent with the general version of the legend, it is not absolutely novel and gives an excuse for Helen's knowing of Achilles—which would otherwise be inexplicable, given her seventeen years' isolation in Egypt.

110 *Another man* Odysseus; see, e.g., Sophocles' *Ajax*, passim.

127 *the gods made you imagine it all* Again, Euripides uses the word *dokēsis;* again we see the emphasis on appearance and reality.

129 We have omitted, with Dale, the two preceding lines (121f. in the Greek text), as being redundant and obscure.

144 *two different rumors* And yet again Euripides cannot resist casting doubt as to what is real, what false.

152 *Theonöe* We must assume that her fame is indeed widespread for Teucer to know of her.

171 *home* Euripides puts it more vividly ("to the streams of Eurotas") from the point of view of his—but not a present-day—audience.

173-270 The first lyric passage, with two strophes and antistrophes followed (244-70) by an epode; as prelude, Helen chants three dactylic lines (173-79 in this translation). The meter, in Greek, is mainly trochaic. Although the text (as all too often in the choruses of the *Helen*) is frequently unclear or corrupt, the sense can normally be ascertained with confidence—which cannot always be said.

181 *you Sirens* Why Sirens? The Sirens are represented in art as winged (women with birds' wings, or birds with human heads), and regularly have a connexion with death: their images were often carved on tombs, and they may even have been painted here on the tomb of Proteus.

193ff. *By the blue pool* This passage (or *parodos,* marking the entry of the Chorus) inevitably recalls the more famous "laundry" scene at *Hippolytus* (121-30).

210 *my ill-used name* The familiar appearance/reality contrast is brought out even in a choric ode, where it might seem especially inappropriate.

238f. *a rumor . . . that implies you sleep* But how could the Chorus know this? Here and elsewhere Euripides is less than careful about what, in the given circumstances, could be known by whom—as, on occasion, things are not known which, since Theonöe is omniscient, really ought to be known. Of course, too much should not be made of this.

243 *Athene's brazen temple* It is worth pointing out that this is the *Spartan* Athene, whose temple was lined with bronze plates; there is a description in Pausanias (3.17.2,3).

270 *in name* Yet again Helen drives the point home.

271-403 The second scene, between Helen and the Chorus.

274 We omit lines 257-59 of the Greek text, with Murray and against Dale, as being "tastelessly grotesque"; but we recognize that, in this play, it is not impossible that Euripides wrote what he is alleged to have done.

299f. *My daughter . . . withers in spinsterhood* Hermione is meant; the exaggeration—Hermione is perhaps nineteen or twenty—is pardonable.

314 Here again we have omitted several lines (299-302 in the Greek) with Murray and Dale; they are silly, tasteless, and questionable Greek—a combination infrequently if ever found in Euripides.

321f. So we translate; but the Greek as transmitted is highly complex and compressed. While the general sense seems clear enough, we suspect corruption. See Dale, *ad loc.* (Greek text, 308-10)

335 Yet again we have omitted (with Dale but against Murray) three lines of the Greek (324-26): "impossible to construe and wholly superfluous" (Dale).

339 At this point, Helen breaks into a lyric dialogue, or *kommos*, with the Chorus, which is followed by a solo lament (373), itself leading into (390) a complex and corrupt passage in a dactylic meter.

365 The Greek at this point (353ff.) is implausible and probably corrupt; see Dale *ad loc.* But the sense, once again, is clear: various methods of suicide (hanging, cutting one's throat) are, not for the first time, being considered.

370 *Priam's boy* Paris.

392 The line of thought here is that other women whose beauty brought them low (Kallisto and the daughter of Merops) were relatively fortunate

compared to Helen, whose beauty destroyed not only her but the Greeks and Trojans as well. But, once again, the Greek as transmitted is at best confused and several readings are doubtful. For example, the reference to Leda in 395 seems irrelevant; while the text implies, too, that Kallisto was transformed into a lion rather than a bear (as is invariably stated elsewhere). The daughter of Merops is unknown; animal metamorphoses are a common thread—but do not apply to Helen. Incongruous as the stanza appears to us, "certainly Euripides," as Dale says, "intends no burlesque here." For another interpretation, see Dale, *Classical Review* (New Series) x (1960), 194-95: lioness = beast generically.

404-538 The third scene: Menelaos and the Portress.

This scene and the following one, with the great hero in rags and being rudely rebuffed by, of all people, a portress, were among those which did no good to Euripides' reputation—at least in the eyes of Aristophanes. It is worth comparing the parody, considerable in length and quoting *in extenso* from *Helen*, which appeared the following year in Aristophanes' *Thesmophoriazūsae*: see 849-918.

462 *look like a Greek*   But how does she know?

507-21 Bemused reflections on his predicament and the possibility of coincidence—what, a *second* Helen, Zeus, Sparta, Tyndareus, Troy? The impression is one of naiveté and bewilderment—with a degree of blustering recovery of confidence in 521ff.

539-922 The fourth scene, extended to the length of an "act" (of course, the Greeks did not think in those terms, nor did time pass between scenes or "acts" as it may well do in a modern play). For a superlative account of how the Greeks handled stagecraft, see *The Stagecraft of Aeschylus*, by Oliver Taplin (Oxford, 1977), or, more accessibly, the same author's *Greek Tragedy in Action* (London, 1978).

This act, including the standard recognition (*anagnōrisis*) scene, is of course one of the central sections of the play. We have Menelaos, Helen, a Messenger, and the Chorus.

539-50 Essential *reportage* by the Chorus—not a full-scale choric ode.

553 *knows the truth of all things* In that case, there is a lot that she has not passed on to Helen!

586 This line does not appear in the manuscripts of Euripides, but is supplied— essentially—from the parody in *Thesmophoriazūsae*.

592ff. Menelaos' bewilderment, remember, is understandable. He has absolutely no reason to believe that this person is the "real" Helen.

601 We omit two otiose lines (following Dale) after this line.

611 *A name* The familiar *onoma-sōma* dichotomy.

615ff. An unexpected end, it seems, to a recognition scene! But help is on the way, via what A. Pippin Burnett has usefully called a "manipulated revelation, so different from an internally necessary discovery of the truth." (*Catastrophe Survived*, Oxford, 1971, p. 84.)

641 *So you've been here* The Servant is understandably annoyed at what he takes for a trick.

651-753 The Recognition Duet is composed in a mixture of meters, including standard iambic trimeters; trimeters are mainly given to the male, lyric meters to the (more emotional) female. The main problem in this scene lies in the ascription of lines to the right speaker; see, especially, G. Zuntz, *Inquiry into the Transmission of the Plays of Euripides* (Cambridge, 1965), chapters 4 and 5. Certainty is, as so often, unattainable, and agreement has not yet been reached. We offer our version with no more than moderate conviction that it approaches what Euripides wrote, and, in particular, draw attention to Anne Pippin Burnett's version of 676ff.:

> MENELAOS But this splendid disaster has brought me to you—a tardy husband, indeed, but all the same, I mean to enjoy my luck!
>
> HELEN *Do, by all means!* I pray for the same thing that you do; it would be wrong, in a married pair, for one to suffer when the other was content.
>
> (*Catastrophe Survived*, p. 85)

Burnett's view is that this is an "erotic *sous-entendu*."

655 Taplin (*Greek Tragedy in Action*, p. 72) well comments:

> Recognition scenes naturally culminate in the heartwarming *embrace* of the long-separated kin, and in Greek tragedy this is usually the cue for a lyric duet which squeezes the last tear from this favourite episode. But before this satisfaction is allowed the recognition is often long delayed by incredulity, misunderstanding, the production of proof and so on. The plays where the embrace is most skilfully delayed and the longing for reunion most tantalizingly drawn out are probably Euripides' *Iphigenia* (*among the Taurians*) and *Helen*.

679 Whether Helen or Menelaos should be speaking here, it is at least clear that we should not (as Murray does) attribute the lines to the Chorus.

754 The action resumes.

767 Note the homely thoughts, the limited perspectives of the stunned but loyal servant—and his more telling remarks which will follow shortly.

803-5 The Greek as transmitted contains some hopelessly otiose material; we have omitted, with J. Jackson (*Marginalia Scaenica*, Oxford, 1955, p. 240) part of lines 741-42 of the Greek text.

806ff. Why this sudden attack by the Servant on the art of prophecy? Most obviously, because Euripides wished to lash out at divination and the important part it had been playing in the contemporary scene—especially before and during the Sicilian Expedition (Thucydides, viii. 1). Dale points out that Euripides attacks divination elsewhere (*Electra, Phoenissae, Bacchae*, the two *Iphigeneias*) in unvarying tones of hostility and contempt.

More particularly, here, we may feel (with Burnett, *op. cit.*, p. 87) that these are reflections on the result of the gods' deceit as the first fact of one's universe. In that case, prophecy will not help—rather, lead your life according to the most sensible rules of mortal men. Which is not to say that Euripides was not riding a favorite hobby horse at a time when his views would be likely to command exceptionally widespread consent.

826 With the end of the Recognition Scene, the action moves on toward the Intrigue (843ff.).

832 As a result of the treacherous murder of Palamedes at Troy, his father Nauplios had lit misleading beacons in revenge on a promontory of Euboia

in order to lure the Greek ships to destruction. Plays were written on this subject by both Euripides and Sophocles, but neither survives.

834 *Perseus' look-out rock*   According to Herodotus (ii. 15) this place marks the western limit of the Nile Delta, corresponding to the modern Aboukir. Here Andromeda was chained to her rock.

887 *An oracular-sounding name*   Because Theonöe (see 13ff.) means, roughly, "knowing divine designs."

914-15 *when Nestor/was left without a son*   The death of Antilochos is meant, cf. *Odyssey* 4.187.

932-1185 The fifth "act" or scene: the nomenclature is irrelevant, but this is the central and crucial hinge of the play, on which all else depends. The presence of Theonöe lifts the action to a new plane of seriousness, and Theonöe's speeches are composed in a Greek altogether more elevated than is the case elsewhere in the play. Theonöe's character and language stand in sharp relief to those of the other *dramatis personae*; here at least, and at last, there is no sense of the comic or burlesque. Nor does Aristophanes ever quote from her.

946 *This day the assembly of the gods*   She is indeed well informed; the implication of Dale's note *ad loc.* (Greek 878f.) is that Euripides was, consciously or unconsciously, transferring the scene in the epic mode to Olympus, where it would all be described in *oratio recta* and in full.

963ff. In the more usual version of what follows, the arbiter would be asked to consider his or her verdict on two different and opposing pleas. Here, of course, two people plead for the same decision, but in two wholly different ways.

1014 *The words you have spoken*   Who speaks *these* words? The problem is a delicate one. Murray gives them to the Chorus; Pearson (C.U.P., 1903) similarly. Dale (at line 945 in the Greek) follows the manuscript tradition in giving them to Theonöe. This divergence highlights one of the difficulties facing modern editors or translators of Greek dramatists: who is speaking at a given moment? (Our manuscript traditions of who is speaking are the result of later scholarship. Papyrus discoveries show that scribes normally marked changes of speaker only by a *paragraphos* (—) or *dikolon* (:), both of which are sigla easily omitted.) In a case like this, it has to be asked how far back our tradition extends; and ultimately we have nothing better to go on than our own sense of the fitting, itself partly influenced by more or less parallel cases. Burnett (*op. cit.*, p. 90) reminds us, with justice, that "the two-line (here, three-line) interruption that in a sense passes the speaker's wand from one character to another is a commonplace with the chorus, and so is this kind of frank curiosity (cf. e.g. [Aesch.] *P.V.* 631), whereas there is no precedent for such a speech from the magisterial figure in this kind of scene." Moreover, as she points out, Athene never once interrupts while the two parties in the *Eumenides* are in debate in the trial scene there. As usual, there are arguments on both sides; we feel more comfortable, *pace* Dale, in attributing the lines to the Chorus. That said, it seems only fair to report Dale's comment: "both [Theonöe's] silence and the Chorus's speech (at least in these terms) would be impossibly bad-mannered." (We, not Burnett, bracket the name of Aeschylus above.)

1017ff. The blustering speech of Menelaos, wholly in keeping with his character as displayed in the *Helen*, must have been a severe test of Theonöe's patience. He even ends (1050ff.) by threats of murder (of Helen and Theoklymenos, Theonöe's brother) and suicide. It is not until he is seen from afar (later on, in the Messenger's speech) that Menelaos regains anything like his heroic stature.

1072-91 There is no more solemn or moving speech in the play; and in it (besides the striking "shrine of Justice," 1076), 1089-91 are especially worthy of remark, as implying life after death in a way more reminiscent of later religions than is commonly associated with Athens of the fifth century B.C. Dale says that the passage does not go far as "an anticipation of the Platonic doctrine of rewards and punishments after death and of the immortality of the soul" but rather is a "piece of high-toned but vague mysticism appropriate to Theonöe." And, of course, it would be quite inappropriate to draw any inference from this passage as to Euripides' beliefs, if any, in a future state. Rather, Theonöe here is making an abstract of religious speculation, past and present—and to come. What would be intriguing to know is whether there had been an upsurge of this kind of "theological" speculation following the enormous casualty lists of the Sicilian expedition; do Theonöe's words link in any way with the Servant's earlier diatribe on prophecy? After castigating the Athenians for their gullibility over divination, is he now giving them a sop via a promise of a kind of immortality? Probably not: there is a remarkably similar passage at Euripides, *Supplices*, 531-4, and the idea may have been a philosophical commonplace of the time.

1115ff. Menelaos' ideas for their escape are characterized, it will be seen, by their extreme implausibility.

1132 *old-fashioned*   The immediate reference is probably to Sophocles' *Electra*, 56-64, where a similar idea is pondered over; as Dale says, the comment is a "rather mischievous interpolation" by Euripides. It is perfectly possible that Sophocles' *Electra* had appeared in the previous year.

1178 *my name, not me*   Once again, the Greek has *onoma* and *sōma* in close juxtaposition.

1186-1252 After the great central scenes of the play—the Recognition, the Trial (or *agōn*), the Intrigue—comes at last relief in the form of a long choral ode; as Dale says, the *first proper stasimon* of the play.

This *stasimon*, in the fourth stanza (1240ff.), contains the only explicit attack on war in the play. But, of course, implicit throughout is the anti-war atmosphere resulting from the knowledge that the Trojan War was fought for a phantom. Had not the Athenians first seen their own dream of Western expansion vanish hideously at Syracuse?

1191 *brown, rippling*   The Greek word is *xouthos*, which, like some other Greek words, manages to combine several notions in one—color, sound, and movement.

1208 *Nauplios*   See note on 832.

1221ff. There are many textual uncertainties in this and the following stanza, and at times even the sense required cannot be established with confidence.

1257-1390 The sixth scene; Helen, Theoklymenos, and Menelaos.

1257-60 The effect, to a modern audience, of these lines is likely to be one of awkwardness, even naiveté.

1292 Note the double meaning. This scene allows maximum scope for such word play, with Helen frequently saying one thing and meaning another: very typical Euripides.

1294 *cowering* Poor Menelaos! Cowering, in rags, written off as dead.

1377 *Crying* We have adopted J. Jackson's admirable emendation (*Marginalia Scaenica* (Oxford, 1955), 131ff.), of *gooîs* (crying) for the otiose *posis* (husband).

1391-1459 The second *stasimon:*
It is hard to connect the story of the Great Mother, Demeter, plausibly in any way with the *Helen*. At the risk of seeming disrespectful to Euripides, we have even ventured to wonder whether this lyric ("perhaps reflecting something of the style of contemporary dithyramb"—Dalè) was not, so to speak, in Euripides' stockpile and brought out here to fill the gap. Although a tenuous connection with Helen emerges in the final stanza, the ode stands on its own. The final stanza, it should be added, has come down to us in a particularly poor state.
Dale, p. 147, comments usefully on the content of the ode, saying (*inter alia*) that "this is the most explicit indication we have in literature of the process of syncretism at work in fifth-century Greece." Here the din and wildness of Phrygian cults are grafted on to the myth of the sorrowing Demeter. Verrall's argument (Introduction, p. 17) makes good use of this stasimon.

1400 *car* The Greek word, *satinē*, is relatively unusual and probably an import from the East.

1448 *you failed to honor the name* So we render the corrupt and obscure Greek. Whether Helen's offense was one of commission or omission is impossible to determine; we have followed Dale's approach.

1460-1549 The seventh scene: Theoklymenos, Helen, Menelaos.
It is unclear at what point Menelaos enters this scene; it must

always be remembered that our only indications of who is on the stage of a Greek play at any moment come from the text itself. Here a lacuna has been posited after 1464 (which might have provided us with the answer); otherwise, we must wait for 1470. The words which we have rendered "So here he comes" could as well bear the sense, in effect, "So here he is"; but it seems to us perhaps more likely that he enters with Theoklymenos and the attendants. These dramaturgical points are of importance everywhere, but especially at places like this where they affect one's judgment of the play's degree of humor: is Menelaos being pointed to or talked about?

1550-1608 The third *stasimon*: the meter, as in the preceding stasimon, is predominantly aeolo-choriambic (Dale, p. 158). Textually this ode is perhaps less obscure and corrupt than the others.

1560 *the city that Perseus founded* Mycenae—but not specifically intended as the point of disembarkation.

1565-67 *the boy whom . . . Apollo killed* Hyacinthos.

1607-8 These lines are very reminiscent of what remains to us of Stesichorus' *palinode* (see Introduction, p. 4).

1609-1791 The eighth, and final, scene or "act": Theoklymenos, Messenger, Dioskouroi, Chorus.

1613 Ironic, and rather reminiscent of the Servant's words at 644.

1623-1715 This superb Messenger's speech deserves the closest attention; in force, speed, directness, vigor it ranks with the very best of Euripides. There are occasional textual problems, but these cannot obscure the splendid liveliness with which the tale of deceit and disaster is unfolded.

1631f. A passage of notorious difficulty and corruption: we are fairly confident of having provided the sense required by the context.

1661 It must have been a very small bull. After 1664, the Greek appears to refer to a horse as well; but this animal makes no subsequent appearance of any kind, and we have banished it back to the mind of

the interpolator whence it sprang. There is no room for superfluous material in so taut and dramatic a narration.

1687 *Row about to the right*   A probable interpretation of a vexed passage.

1716 The nervous disingenuousness of the Chorus is, to say the least of it, understandable.

1718ff. From here to 1739 the meter changes to the trochaic tetrameter catalectic—
a vigorous rhythm which also allows the rapid interchange be-
tween Theoklymenos and the Chorus to take place within the
confines of single lines.

1740 The *deus* (or, rather, *dei*) *ex machina* makes a timely appearance.

1771 An example of Euripides' favorite practice of explanatory rationalization. The
long island which guards the coast of Attica (here called Actē in
the Greek) is Makronnisi, off Sounion.

1776 The most promising and plausible meaning of the line, but one which is
difficult to extract from the Greek.

1785-91 The anapestic finale of *Alcestis, Andromache, Bacchae,* and (almost)
Medea; the equivalent of ringing down the curtain—the Chorus
leaves the Orchestra.

GLOSSARY

ACHAEAN, synonym for Greek in Homer and later writers. Achaia was originally a region including southeast Thessaly and part of the northern Peloponnese.

ACHILLES, greatest warrior among the Greeks at Troy, Prince of Phthia, and suitor of Helen. His quarrel with Agamemnon and its consequences are the subject of the *Iliad* of Homer. See also THETIS. Family Tree 7.

AEGEAN, sea between Greece and Asia Minor. The Greeks derived its name from Aegeus, King of Athens and father of Theseus, who drowned himself in it.

AEROPE, Family Tree 2.

AGAMEMNON, King of Mycenae and traditionally supreme captain of the Greeks at Troy. On his return he was murdered by Clytemnestra and her lover Aegisthos. Family Tree 2.

AIAKOS, King of Aegina. Because of his outstanding piety he was made a judge of souls and keeper of the keys of Hades on his death. Family Tree 7.

AJAX (AIAS), famous leader of the Salaminians at Troy. He killed himself out of rage at the award of Achilles' arms to Odysseus, another Greek captain. See Family Tree 7.

ALEXANDER, see PARIS.

APHRODITE, daughter of Zeus and Dione, goddess of love and giver of gaiety, beauty, and all attractions which inspire it. She represents irrational overwhelming passion, which runs counter to the moderation admired by the Greeks. After a quarrel had broken out at the wedding of Peleus and

Thetis among Aphrodite, Athene, and Hera about which of them was the most beautiful, Hermes brought the goddesses to Paris on Mount Ida for him to judge. Aphrodite won by offering him Helen as a bribe. In this way she caused the Trojan War (see HELEN).

APOLLO, son of Zeus and Leto, twin brother of Artemis, god of music, the sun and prophecy—especially at his oracle in Delphi. See also HYACINTHOS.

ARCADIA, mountainous region of the central Peloponnese, inhabited by peoples with a pastoral way of life.

ARGOS, poetic synonym for Greece. Argos was a city on the east coast of Greece, and, more generally, the area under Agamemnon's rule.

ARTEMIS, virgin goddess of the hunt, fertility and the wilderness. See APOLLO.

ATHENE, favorite daughter of Zeus. She is said to have sprung, fully armed, from his head, but she is warlike only in protection of her chosen heroes and cities, especially Athens. Athene is also the virgin goddess of wisdom, crafts, and birds.

ATREUS, King of Mycenae. He served up the flesh of the children of his brother, Thyestes, at a banquet in revenge for Thyestes' theft of a golden ram, which was an heirloom of their house. See Family Tree 2.

CRETE, island in the Aegean.

CYPRIS, title of Aphrodite from her famous shrine in Cyprus.

CYPRUS, island at extreme eastern end of the Mediterranean.

DANAOS, King of Argos. For this reason "Danaan" is a synonym for "Argive" and hence for "Greek." Family Tree 5.

DARDANOS, ancestor of Priam and founder of Troy. Family Tree 4.

DIOSKOUROI, the Heavenly Twins who sailed with Jason in the Argo, rescued Helen from Theseus, and were eventually transformed by Zeus into the constellation of Gemini. The story that they killed themselves for their sister's shame is Euripides' invention. See also LEUKIPPIDES, LEDA. Family Tree 3.

EGYPT, westernmost of the African lands on the Mediterranean, nearest to Greece but an exotic and little-known country to the ancient Greeks.

EIDO, see THEONÖE.

ENODIA, title of Hekate (the Roadside Goddess) from her shrines at crossroads.

EUBOIA, large island on eastern coast of Greece.

EUROTAS, river of Sparta.

GALENEIA, a sea-nymph personifying calm.

GORGOPIS, title of Athene, meaning "of the terrible eyes."

GRACES, daughters of Zeus and attendants of Aphrodite. They were the three goddesses of charm and beauty.

GREAT MOTHER (Demeter), goddess of agriculture and fertility. Euripides gives her the attendant wild beasts and mountain home of the Phrygian earth-goddess Kybele. See PHERSEPHASSA.

HADES, brother of Zeus and king of the Underworld, which often bears his name. It was set in the center of the earth below the region of darkness called Erebus. There souls after death led a shadowy existence with no pleasure or pain. Only the outstandingly wicked were punished in Tartarus, and only heroes were permitted to enter Elysium or the Isles of the Blest.

HEKATE, goddess of the Underworld, of the moon, and of magic, often attended by phantoms and ghosts. See also ENODIA.

HELEN, the most beautiful woman in the world, especially admired by the Greeks for her blond hair. Many of the greatest men in Greece were her suitors, and swore to support her husband, whoever he might be. Thus Paris' kidnapping of her from Sparta, with Aphrodite's help, led to an expedition against Troy, drawn from all Greece. After her death she was made divine, as were her brothers. See also APHRODITE, MENELAOS, LEDA. Family Trees 2 and 3.

HELENOS, Trojan warrior and prophet. Family Tree 4.

HELLAS, The Greeks' own name for their country (and hence, Hellēnes for themselves). It was originally part of South Thessaly.

HERA, goddess of marriage and all female concerns, wife and sister of Zeus, of whose mistresses and their children she is always jealous.

HERMES, son of Zeus and Maia—Arcadian god of travelers and merchants, guide of souls to Hades but especially messenger of the gods.

HERMIONE, Family Tree 2.

HYACINTHOS, son of Amyelas of Lakonia, eponym of Amyelai where his festival is celebrated. Boreas, the North Wind, and Zephyrus, the West Wind, jealous of Apollo's love for him, blew so hard while he and Apollo were competing with a discus, that Apollo's discus hit and killed him. Where his blood touched the ground, the hyacinth sprang up.

IDA (MOUNT), wooded mountain near Troy; there was another mountain, of the same name, in Crete.

ILION, see TROY.

KALCHAS, prophet who accompanied the Greeks to Troy.

KALLISTO, Arcadian nymph, loved by Zeus, whom Hera turned into a bear out of jealousy. Zeus eventually set her among the stars as the constellation of the Great Bear.

KAPHEREOS, town in Euboeia.

KASTOR, see DIOSKOUROI.

LAKEDAIMON, usual name in prose for Sparta.

LAKONIA, a region under Spartan rule.

LEDA, said to have laid the eggs from which Helen and her brothers were hatched after Zeus had come to her in the shape of a swan. Helen herself, reflecting the scepticism of later Greeks, prefers Tyndareus as her father. Family Tree 3.

LEUKIPPIDES, Phoebe and Hilaira, daughters of Leukippus. According to one story, the Dioskouroi carried them off and were killed as they fled by Leukippus' nephews.

LIBYA, Greek name for Africa.

MAIA, one of the Pleiades and mother of Hermes by Zeus.

MENELAOS, King of Sparta. Euripides makes him leader of the Greeks and sacker of Troy (see AGAMEMNON) but follows the Odyssey in the Dioskouroi's promise of Elysium (see HADES). He is said to have tried to kill Helen at the sack of Troy before she persuaded him to a reconciliation. Family Tree 2.

MEROPS, King of Ethiopia.

MUSES, the nine daughters of Zeus and Mnemosyne (Memory), goddesses of literature, music, and dance, attendants of Apollo. (Hence "museum.")

NAIAD, river-nymph, possibly here Syrinx, whom Pan pursued in vain, and so invented his pipes, which he called syringes after her.

NAUPLIA, town near Korinth, named after ancestor of following with the same name.

NAUPLIOS, Greek warrior who helped to wreck the Greek fleet returning from Troy by lighting a false beacon on the cliffs near Kaphereos in Euboia in revenge for the execution of his son Palamedes on evidence planted by Odysseus.

NELEUS, Family Tree 6. Antilochos was killed while defending his ancient father Nestor against Memnon, King of Ethiopia.

NEREUS, wise god of the Aegean sea, who had the gift of prophecy. Family Tree 1.

NILE, river of Egypt. Euripides gives Anaxagoras' guess about the annual flooding: the main cause is in fact the summer rains on the Abyssinian plateau.

NYMPHS, female nature-spirits, usually young and beautiful.

OINOMAOS, King of Pisa, a town east of Olympia in the Peloponnese. He pursued and killed all suitors of his daughter, as there was a prophecy that her husband would kill him, which was fulfilled when, in pursuit of Pelops, he was thrown from his chariot. See also PELOPS. Family Tree 2.

ORION, Boeotian giant and great hunter. He was eventually turned into a constellation with his dog, Sirios.

PALLAS, title of Athene.

PAN, Arcadian son of Hermes; a rustic shepherd god who could inspire a feeling of "panic."

PARIS, Hecuba had an ominous dream while carrying him, and the child was exposed. He was found and brought up by shepherds on Mount Ida. Paris died in the sack of Troy. See also HELEN, APHRODITE. Family Tree 4.

PELEUS, after his banishment and adventures in Phthia and Iolchos, he was given Thetis as a reward for his virtue. See also TELEMON, THETIS. Family Tree 7.

PELOPS, won Hippodameia by bribing her father's charioteer to remove the linchpins of his chariot, so that he would not be pursued. See also TANTALOS, OINOMAOS. Family Tree 2.

PERSEUS, Arisius, King of Argos, shut Danaë up in a subterranean prison after the oracle of Delphi had declared that her son would kill him, but Perseus was born after Zeus had visited her in a shower of gold. After killing the Gorgon Medusa with the help of Hermes and Athena, and rescuing Andromeda from a sea-monster, he returned to Argos and fulfilled the prophecy by accident.

PHAROS, an island in the bay of Alexandria at the mouth of the Nile, later famous for its lighthouse.

PHERSEPHASSA (or PERSEPHONE), daughter of Demeter, carried off to the Underworld from among her friends by Hades. Demeter wandered over the earth, searching for her, and not allowing anything to grow, or the streams to run, until Zeus decreed that Phersephassa must return. But as she had eaten some pomegranate seeds, Persephone must stay part of the year in Hades as Queen of the Dead. Her name was never spoken so as not to reawaken Demeter's grief.

PHOENICIA, coastal strip of Syria at the extreme western end of the Mediterranean, country of the greatest trading and seafaring nation known to the Greeks.

PHOIBOS, title of Apollo in his aspect as god of the sun.

PHRYGIAN, synonym for Trojan. Phrygia was part of central and western Asia Minor.

PISA, kingdom of Oinomaos near Olympia in Greece.

PLEIADES, seven sisters who appealed to Zeus when Orion pursued them, and were turned into stars.

PLOUTOS, riches personified.

PONTOS, the open sea personified. Family Tree 1.

POSEIDON, brother of Zeus, god of earthquakes, horses, and above all, the sea.

PRIAM, King of Troy, famous for his piety and wisdom. He was killed in the sack of the city. Family Tree 4.

PROTEUS, King of Egypt, though he appears in the Odyssey as a minor sea-god. Family Tree 1.

PSAMATHE, a sea-nymph. Family Trees 1 and 7.

SALAMIS, 1. island in the bay of Eleusis, originally a possession of Aegina, kingdom of Telamon.

2. Greek capital of Cyprus, kingdom of Teucer.

SIDON, great Phoenician city on the Syrian coast.

SIMOIS, river of Troy.

SIRENS, chthonian goddesses, half-woman, half-bird, who charmed sailors onto their island by their song so that they could devour them. They also accompany the dead to Hades and mourn for them and for Phersephassa.

SKAMANDER, river of Troy, also called Xanthos.

SPARTA, poetic synonym for Lakedaimon, a Dorian city in the Peloponnese.

TANTALOS, served up his son to the Gods at a banquet to see if they would realize what they were eating. He was punished in Tartarus (see HADES) by being made to stand, hungry and thirsty, up to his chin in water, with fruit hanging over his head, only to have it move out of his reach whenever he tried to eat or drink—hence "tantalize." Family Tree 2.

TELAMON, banished with Peleus from Aegina by Aiakos for killing Phokos. He settled in Salamis. Family Tree 7.

TEUCER, banished by Telamon from Salamis for returning from Troy without his brother (see AIAS). He founded Salamis in Cyprus by Apollo's direction. Family Tree 7.

THEOKLYMENOS, King of Egypt and a hater of Greeks. Family Tree 1.

THEONÖE, virgin prophetess. Family Tree 1.

THESTIOS, King of Aitolia. Family Tree 3.

THETIS, a sea-nymph fated to bear a son greater than his father. When they discovered this, Zeus and Poseidon gave up their courtships of her and bestowed her on Peleus. She left Peleus for interfering when she was dipping Achilles in the Styx, a river of Hades, to make him immortal. For this reason, Achilles' heel, by which she was holding him, remained vulnerable, and he died when Paris' arrow wounded it. Family Tree 7.

TROY, city in Asia Minor close to the western entrance to the Dardanelles, sacked by the Greeks after ten years' siege. See also HELEN, APHRODITE.

TYNDAREUS, King of Sparta. Family Tree 3.

ZEUS, "father of gods and men" in the Homeric formula. The supreme god of the Greeks, whose home was on Mount Olympos, the highest mountain in Greece. His will is identified with destiny; he is the maintainer of law and morality and hence protector of the weak. But he has other aspects as the lover of innumerable goddesses, nymphs, and mortals, the god of the weather, and the king of the large and disobedient community of the gods.